Computer Operating Systems

FOR MICROS, MINIS AND MAINFRAM

Computer Operating Systems

FOR MICROS, MINIS AND MAINFRAMES

David Barron

Professor of Computer Studies
University of Southampton

SECOND EDITION

LONDON   NEW YORK

Chapman and Hall

First published 1971 by
Chapman and Hall Ltd
11 New Fetter Lane, London EC4P 4EE
Reprinted 1973, 1975
Second edition 1984
Reprinted 1987
Published in the USA by
Chapman and Hall
29 West 35th Street, New York NY 10001

Printed in Great Britain by
J.W. Arrowsmith Ltd., Bristol

ISBN 0 412 15620 2 (hardback)
ISBN 0 412 15630 X (paperback)

British Library Cataloguing in Publication Data

Barron, D.W.
   Computer operating systems.—2nd ed.—
   (Chapman and Hall computing)
   1. Operating systems (Computers)
   I. Title
   001.64'25   QA76.6

   ISBN 0–412–15620–2
   ISBN 0–412–15630–X Pbk

Library of Congress Cataloging in Publication Data

Barron, D. W. (David William), 1935–
   Computer operating systems.

   Includes index.
   1. Operating systems (Computers) I. Title.
QA76.6.B37   1984   001.64'2   84–9537
ISBN 0–412–15620–2
ISBN 0–412–15630–X (pbk.)

Contents

Preface

This book is based on my earlier text, *Computer Operating Systems*, written in 1970. In the preface to that book I remarked that '. . .up to the present, development (of operating systems) has been of a largely *ad hoc* and pragmatic nature, and has been aptly characterized as "moderate success at enormous expense" '. Thirteen years later the picture is not much different so far as mainframe systems are concerned. Thousands of man-years have gone into the development of systems like IBM's VMS and ICL's VME, producing systems that occupy prodigious amounts of memory, soak up processor cycles, and require an army of systems programmers to 'maintain' them. Truly it has been said that, 'an elephant is a mouse with an IBM operating system'. While this investment means that systems of this kind will be with us for many years to come, they are in some way the end of the line, and will come to be seen as an evolutionary dead-end.

Looking at these over-large and excessively complicated systems, one cannot help feeling that there must be a better way of doing things, and driven by the very different requirements of small machines a new breed of operating system has developed for mini- and microcomputers, quite unlike the traditional variety. The emphasis in this book is largely on these new operating systems, in keeping with my view that the mainframe has had its day, and that the future lies with the micro. However, the older systems are by no means ignored since there is much to be learned from a study of the past, in computing as in any other subject.

With an increasing understanding of operating systems we see more clearly their underlying structure, and this text is more concerned with the way operating systems can now be constructed than with the sordid details of the internal economy of the older systems. Moreover, it is not a theoretical text: it remains sufficiently close to the realities of modern-day operating systems to give the reader an appreciation of why things are as they are, as well as how they might be.

Whatever kind of computer system is used, an operating system is likely to loom large in the user's view. Thus, not only students and computer specialists, but also anyone interested in how computer systems work, needs to know about operating systems. It is my aim to convey 'what everyone in computing should know about operating systems'. I hope that Computer Operating Systems will be of use in introductory courses, and will also be of interest to all computer users, including the growing army of amateurs who find in computing an absorbing hobby.

David Barron

1
Some background

1.1 WHAT THE OPERATING SYSTEM DOES

Almost without exception, every computer has an operating system. The reasons for having one, and the particular kind of system, are very different on different varieties of machine, but the operating system is always there. Indeed, to most users the operating system *is* the machine. They never see a 'raw' machine: instead they see and use the interface presented by the operating system.

A 'raw' machine is a most inhospitable device. In order to do anything, it requires a program in a specific binary representation of the particular machine code. In particular it needs more-or-less complicated programs to drive its peripherals before it can even communicate with the outside world. It is therefore usual to provide *system software* to make the system usable. In a home computer this system software is an integral part of the system, contained in a read-only memory (ROM) and automatically entered when the system is switched on. Thus the user does not distinguish between the CPU (central processing unit) and the operating system: they combine to provide a programming environment in which programs (usually in BASIC) can be run, saved on cassette tape and later reloaded. In large personal computers (e.g. the IBM PC) and in minicomputers and mainframes we can identify a number of individual pieces of system software, mostly concerned with program preparation – editors, assemblers, compilers, link-editors, etc. Pervading all these is the operating system. It has been described as the 'glue' which holds all the other components together. Alternatively we can view it as providing an infrastructure: a common environment in which the various system programs can operate, including the mechanisms for communicating with the peripheral devices. (From the early days, some of the complexity of controlling input/output devices had been concealed from the user by the provision of a software package called the Input–Output Control System (IOCS), and with the trend in early computers to have I/O functions controlled partly by hardware and partly by software, a natural development was to incorporate the IOCS into the operating system.)

This is a relatively modern view of operating systems, which were originally developed in response to a quite different need – to maximize the utilization of the central processor and peripheral devices. We must remember that the early computers were phenomenally expensive, and so could not be allowed to be idle. It was therefore necessary to automate the flow of work, and bring decisions on the management of system resources on to the time-scale of the computer rather than that of the human operator. Falling hardware costs removed the preoccupation with 100% processor utilization, but at the same time the typical mode of usage of computers changed, with more emphasis being placed on simultaneous access by a large number of users. Thus the operating system now had to manage the sharing of resources among the users.

As the need to optimize utilization has diminshed, another aspect of the operating system has become of increasing significance: the software interface. Increasing complexity of computer systems led to further functions being incorporated in the operating system to aid the user – for example, organizing disc storage so that it appears as a logical file-structure to the user, unconstrained by the physical organization of tracks, sectors and blocks. The operating system can thus have two distinct facets: on the one hand controlling the allocation and utilization of shared resources, and on the other hand providing an interface to the hardware more convenient and amenable than that presented by the naked machine. This duality of purpose is characteristic of any multi-user operating system, and we will find the same structure in the operating systems both of mainframes and of multi-user minis.

We can thus define the function of an operating system as being to provide a convenient environment for the user(s) of a computer system, whatever their requirements – program development, real-time process control, database management, payroll or whatever. In the case of a personal computer, there is only one user, and the sole function of the operating system is to implement the user-interface. In the case of a multi-user system the operating system must share the resources so as to provide the user-interface to each of the users. Instead of optimizing the utilization of the processor, the aim is to optimize the productivity of the user.

The provision by the operating system of a convenient software environment has had a dramatic effect on the development of personal computers. In the heyday of mainframes and minis, the software was provided by the manufacturer and (to a lesser extent) by the installation's systems programmers, and applications programs were not expected to be portable between machines. In the microcomputer world, however, the situation is different. Software is sold 'off the shelf', and users shop around for the package that best suits their requirements. The situation was bedevilled by incompatible file formats and programming systems until an operating system called CP/M became the *de facto* standard for 8-bit micros, ensuring that programs written to the CP/M interface could be run on most microcomputers.

1.2   KERNEL AND SUPERSTRUCTURE

In discussing operating systems it is convenient to separate those parts which provide the user environment from those parts more directly concerned with sharing resources and interfacing to the machine hardware, such as interrupt handling, storage management, processor scheduling, etc. This latter area we will describe as the *kernel*, and the remainder we call the *superstructure*. On this definition the superstructure comprises those parts of the operating system that provide the basis of services to the user (filing system, command language, etc.), but does not include system software such as editors (which we regard as applications programs). Many older systems include the editor as part of the operating system, but this is not a good feature, since it makes it impossible for the user to take advantage of new developments – he is stuck with the system editor.

The distinction between kernel and superstructure is a particularly useful one to make. It allows the description of a general-purpose operating system to be divided into two parts with a clean interface – as long as one understands *what* the kernel does, one can follow an explanation of the superstructure without needing to know *how* the kernel does its job. Also, the distinction allows us to categorize neatly the operating systems of smaller machines. Thus many minis have an operating system (typically described as a 'resource-sharing executive') which consists almost entirely of kernel, with a very minimal superstructure. DEC's RSX11-M is a typical example of this category of operating system. Personal computers, on the other hand, have a rudimentary operating system that is almost entirely superstructure – since most resources are dedicated to a single purpose there is little for the kernel to do apart from interrupt handling. (What we have just said about single-user systems applies strictly only to single-user single-process systems, in which the single user can do only one thing at once. More advanced single-user systems (e.g. Concurrent CP/M-86) allow the user to set up a number of tasks to run in parallel. In such a system resource allocation once more becomes a necessary function of the operating system.)

1.3   DATA MANAGEMENT AND JOB CONTROL

The major facilities offered by the superstructure are data management and job control. An important part of data managment is the control of the input–output devices. However, there is more to data management than this. The operating system must map logical file structures on to physical devices, and provide *access methods* whereby particular records of a file can be accessed without having to specify at user level the details of file structure and disc layout. If information in files is subject to frequent amendment the system must also take necessary steps to preserve the integrity of the stored information. The operating system can also provide a degree of device-independence, so that the user can see the same logical file structure, independent of the particular devices used for storing his files.

Job control is concerned with executing the user's programs. For a single-user system, or a multi-user on-line terminal system, this requires a command interpreter which accepts commands from the keyboard and performs the operations requested. Job control becomes much more complex in a 'batch' system where users submit jobs to be run without intervention. (For this purpose we define a job as the basic independent unit of work submitted to the machine, i.e. a unit that is neither connected with any other unit of work, nor dependent on any other unit for its completion.) A job will frequently (in fact usually) be composed of job-steps, e.g. compile, link-edit, run. The system must allow the user to link together any number of operations as job-steps, providing the right environment and resources for each step and organizing the passing of files from one job-step to another. It must also be possible to make execution a job-step conditional on the successful running of earlier steps, and even to specify alternative sequences dependent on the outcome of earlier job-steps. For full generality it is desirable for the user to be able to specify steps that can be performed simultaneously, and to be able to synchronize such parallel execution.

1.4   CATEGORIES OF OPERATING SYSTEM

In conclusion we define a few terms that are used to categorize operating systems.

Single user and *multi-user* are self-explanatory.

A *multi-programming* system is one in which the available processor(s) is shared (by the operating system) amongst several programs co-resident in main memory, in order to improve CPU utilization.

A *foreground–background* system is a single-user sytem in which two programs are multi-programmed. One (the foreground) interacts with the terminal and runs as long as it is able; the background program is assigned to the processor whenever the foreground program is unable to proceed (e.g. because it is waiting for the user to do something). As soon as the foreground job is free to proceed it does so. A foreground–background system is a particular case of a single-user multi-process system.

A *concurrent* or *multi-tasking* system is a generalization of a foreground–background system in which the user of a single-user system can initiate a number of concurrent jobs, assigning the terminal display to any one of the jobs as required. (But note that older texts use the term 'multi-tasking' with the meaning here ascribed to multi-programming. Computer terminology is a minefield.)

A *time-sharing* system shares the processor and memory amongst a number of programs, each associated with a remote interactive terminal, in such a way that each user thinks he has a machine to himself.

A *transaction-processing* system (TP system) resembles a time-sharing system in that it serves a number of remote terminals. However, whereas in a time-sharing system each remote user is associated with a different program, and is totally independent of the other terminals and programs, in a TP system all the terminals are connected to the same program (or suite of programs). This program accepts *transactions* from its terminals, processes them and sends responses. The classic example of a TP system is an airline reservation system.

Finally, a *general-purpose* system is a multi-user system that combines batch processing, time-sharing and possibly transaction processing in a single (usually large and complex) system.

2
Mainly historical

2.1. THE USE OF HISTORY

In this chapter we trace the development of the 'traditional' batch and
time-sharing systems. In addition to giving an insight into systems that
are widely used at the present time, this historical survey introduces
many of the concepts that came together to form the basis for design
of modern operating systems. The technology of computing changes
rapidly, and today's innovation is tomorrow's museum piece. In many
parts of the subject it is best to dismiss the history and launch straight into
current technology, but in operating systems we can learn by following
the historical development. Seeing this in a modern context provides a
good basis for understanding the complexities of modern operating
systems – today's Concurrent CP-M/86 has a lot in common with yester-
day's multi-programming executive.

2.2. THE EARLY BATCH SYSTEMS

In the early days of computing, the machines were 'hand-operated'.
That is to say, the operator (in those days often the programmer) set up a
job by loading the card-reader, mounting magnetic tapes, etc., and then
started the program by manipulating switches on the console. If the
program called for operator intervention the operator took appropriate
action and restarted the program. Finally, when the job was finished, the
operator dismounted the tapes, unloaded the card reader, removed the
listing from the printer, and then started setting up the next job. Given
the capital cost of a computer in those days, such a method of working
was acceptable only so long as the set-up time was insignificant in
comparison with the run-time of the job. The early computers were so
slow that this was usually the case, but as computer speeds increased,
the ratio of set-up time to run-time grew to unacceptable proportions,
and the need arose to automate the job-to-job transition. The increase in
processing speed also highlighted the disparity between the speed of

operation of the processor and that of the input–output devices. Efforts to remove this mis-match led to two developments. The first was the introduction of the *I/O channel*, which was a piece of hardware to control I/O devices in an autonomous manner. Once started, the channel ran independently of the central processor, thus allowing I/O to be over-lapped with computing. The program could initiate a transfer and at a later time interrogate the channel to determine whether the transfer had been completed. The second development, of greater significance to the development of operating systems, was the introduction of the tech-nique of 'off-lining' I/O. Instead of the computer using the slow peri-pheral devices directly, input was transcribed from cards to magnetic tape, and the program got its input by reading card-images from the tape. Similarly, output was written as card-images or line-images to tape, and these were later transcribed to card punch or printer as appropriate. The off-line transcription to and from tape was initially done by special-purpose hardware, but it was soon found that it was more economic to use a small computer as a 'satellite'. (The large IBM 7090 scientific computer was rarely to be found without an attendant 1401, a small data-processing machine, as a satellite handling its I/O.) Once the principle of off-lining I/O to tape was established, the way was open for the development of an automated job-sequencing system. All that was required was to record a number of jobs (a *batch*) on tape and arrange that instead of the machine stopping at the end of a program, control should revert to an operating system (or *monitor program*) that immediately started the next job. (This is somewhat of an over-simplification, but will suffice for the present.) Probably the first such system was SOS, the Share Operating System devised by the association of users of IBM machines called SHARE. SOS was the forerunner of the classic Fortran Monitor System, FMS. Since such systems executed a batch of jobs on a magnetic tape in automatic sequence, they became generally known as *batch systems*.

This kind of system had two main attributes: it automated the sequenc-ing of jobs, and it fooled programs into thinking that they had a real card-reader and line-printer when in fact their I/O was being off-lined. This latter did not present much difficulty: I/O via an autonomous chan-nel was so complicated that it was in any case carried out by a package of system routines called the I/O Control System (IOCS). The existence of the off-lining process was easily concealed by modifying the appropri-ate IOCS routines. Automating the job sequencing had more substantial implications. It was necessary to ensure that the monitor was entered whenever a program terminated, natually or by reason of error. Thus FMS programmers were instructed never to use STOP but to terminate execution by CALL EXIT. (To this day some FORTRAN systems use

CALL EXIT, though few of the users or implementors appreciate the reason.) Important facts to note at this stage are:

(1) The monitor program must reside in memory, and will make use of the processor whenever it runs. This is an example of the *overheads* that arise from the use of an operating system. When assessing operating systems the magnitude of such overheads is a major consideration.

(2) We have to ensure that the control program is not overwritten by the user program. We also have to ensure that a user program never STOPs, and does all its I/O via the routines of the IOCS. In the early days it was necessary to rely on programmer discipline, but later systems had assistance from the hardware. For safety it is necessary to have such hardware assistance: the minimal requirements are some sort of storage protection, to deal with the overwriting problem, and a distinction between normal mode working, in which some operations cause a trap to the monitor system, and privileged mode working in which anything goes, so that attempts by the program to STOP or initiate I/O activities can be intercepted.

(3) The system must be resilient against badly formed input decks and faulty programs. Thus an incomplete program must not result in the compiler consuming the data cards (or, worse, the next program), and a program must not be allowed to read past the end of its own data. The user must therefore provide *control information* to delimit his program and data. This will take the form of *control cards*, and it will be necessary to have some convention to distinguish these cards. A common convention is to put a special character (e.g. a dollar sign) in the first column. This means that no program or data card can start with this character – an example of the *constraints* that the operating system imposes on the user.

(4) There must be a means of communication between the compiler(s) and the operating system in order to signal compiling errors and inhibit the subsequent running of the job. Some systems dodge this issue by making the compiler(s) part of the operating system. This is a reprehensible practice, since it makes it difficult to incorporate new compilers, and so restricts the user to the designer's choice of language(s).

2.3 SPOOLING SYSTEMS

For a while, systems of the type just outlined reigned supreme. The next development was triggered by the arrival of a new hardware technique, *the interrupt*. The difficulty of synchronizing an autonomous I/O channel has already been noted. The interrupt obviates this difficulty by having the channel signal the computer when it has finished its job, or when an error condition arises that requires program intervention. When an interrupt occurs the hardware preserves the current state (register contents) and enters an *interrupt routine* to deal with the channel. When the channel has been serviced the interrupted program can be resumed, the hardware restoring the register contents before returning control. The whole process is transparent to the interrupted program, which has no knowledge of the interrupt. It is thus possible for a program to keep peripheral devices running at full speed without having to keep a constant check on the process of the I/O transfers. (It is of interest to note that the interrupt is probably the first computing concept not to have been anticipated by Babbage.)

Initially, this technique was used within a single program, but it required skilled programming and it was soon appreciated that better utilization of equipment could be obtained by the technique of *multi-programming*. This is the technique of having several programs simultaneously in memory, so that whenever one program is waiting for a peripheral device another will be able to use the processor. Multi-programming is particularly effective if programs that are peripheral-limited (in the sense that their execution time is determined mainly by the time taken doing input and output) are run at the same time as programs that are processor-intensive. The first computer to introduce this concept was the Ferranti Orion; multi-programming was fully exploited in the Ferranti (later ICL) Atlas machine.

The concept of multi-programming had an important, and perhaps unexpected, application in operating system design. In a classic FMS-type system the satellite computer is peripheral-limited, while the large computer is for the most part processor-limited. There is thus a potential advantage in dispensing with the satellite and instead using a single computer to perform both jobs by means of multi-programming. Since there is no longer a satellite computer there is of course no physical transfer of a batch of jobs. The earliest systems of this kind used tape as a backing store, and thus still processed jobs in batches. With the advent of disc storage the system became a continuous flow or *job-stream* process, but the terminology 'batch-system' still persists.

Systems of this kind are called *spooling systems*. The acronym SPOOL, derived from 'Simultaneous Peripheral Operation On-Line' was coined within IBM, though the technique pre-dates the acronym, being known within Ferranti as 'pseudo-off-line input–output'. The technique of spooling was invented at Manchester University as part of the Atlas Supervisor (which incorporated many other innovations.) That spooling system was tape-based – a triumph of ingenuity over technology – but all subsequent spooling systems have been disc-based. A spectacularly successful early spooling system was IBM's HASP.

A spooling system involves three simultaneous activities: reading card images to disc, running jobs from disc with output to disc, and transcribing line images from disc to printer. The operating system evidently becomes more complex since in addition to all its previous functions it has to simulate concurrent activity with a single processor and memory. The description of the operating system is simplified if we recognize that this simulation of concurrency is a largely self-contained activity, and encapsulate it in a *multi-programming executive*. The benefit of this is that the executive–hardware combination defines an abstract 'machine' that is capable (apparently) of sustaining concurrent activities. We can therefore describe the spooling system in terms of this 'machine' without worrying how concurrency is achieved. This is an example of the 'separation of concerns' that is so important a part of structured design.

2.3.1 The multi-programming executive

We start by describing a simple executive that is capable of running a fixed number of programs in a pseudo-concurrent manner. The first thing to note is that the programs and the executive must share the memory, each being allocated a contiguous area of appropriate size. We say that the memory is *partitioned*. We have to ensure that a program in one partition cannot affect a program in any other partition. Although it is sometimes necessary to try to enforce this by software, for complete safety we require hardware assistance in the form of *memory protection* or *memory mapping*. We shall examine possible protection and mapping techniques later.

In order to implement multi-programming the hardware must provide a *real-time clock* or *interval timer*. This is a device that generates an interrupt after a preset interval: since such clocks are usually driven by the mains frequency the interval will be a multiple of 1/50 second (1/60 second in the USA). If the programs being multi-programmed were completely independent of each other and of external events, the executive would be trivial. We would set the clock to a suitable interval, say 1/10 second, and use the interrupt to switch from one program to the next, so that the programs are run in turn for 1/10 second each. The quickness of the hand deceives the eye and the programs appear to run in parallel.

However, a realistic system is not so simple. Although the programs will be largely independent, they will need to communicate with each other from time to time, and if they are using peripheral devices they will need to communicate with those devices. Thus a program must bs able to make requests to the executive. This is usually done by a special machine instruction called a *trap* or *supervisor call* (SVC). This transfers control to a fixed place in executive (preserving the processor status in the same way as an interrupt), and changes to system mode. The address field of the instruction is used to identify different SVCs, and additional information can be provided in registers. The following is found to be a sufficient set of SVCs to implement a multi-programming executive:

(1) Halt me, and restart when an interrupt is received from a specified device.
(2) Halt me, and restart when asked to do so by another program.
(3) Restart a specified program.

Further, for complete generality we must allow a priority ordering on the programs. This is necessary to take account of the fact that some I/O devices have a *critical time*, i.e. data must be sent to or taken from the device within a fixed time interval if it is not to be lost. For example, if we are reading data from a cassette tape, the processor must accept the data as it comes from the tape, since the tape is moving at a constant rate and cannot be stopped. An interrupt from the cassette drive must be attended to within this critical time if data is not to be lost, and it follows that the program controlling this device should have higher priority than programs controlling less time-critical devices. (We assume for the sake of argument that the tape is being read on an interrupt basis and is not using DMA (Direct Memory Access) hardware.) In the context of the early spooling systems, it was the card-reader which had a critical time, since the mechanical organization required cards to pass the reading head at a constant rate.

At any time a program in a given partition can be in one of three mutually-exclusive states:

(1) Running.
(2) Free, i.e. able to run if the processor were allocated to it.
(3) Halted, i.e. waiting for a signal from a device or another program.

At the heart of the executive is a *scheduler*. The aim of the scheduler is to ensure that the processor is always allocated to the program of highest priority amongst those not halted.

Associated with each program is a *program control block* whose structure is illustrated in Fig. 2.1. The blocks are chained in order of priority. Whenever anything occurs to change the state of a program the scheduler is entered after the change of state has been made. A simple scan of the chain will locate the highest priority program free to run, and the processor is allocated to this program. This scheduling strategy ensures that if a high-priority program is freed it will be run in preference to a program of lower priority that was running before: this is called *pre-emptive* scheduling. Note that this pre-emption of the processor is

program - id
priority
state
space for register dump etc.
chain

Fig. 2.1   The program control block.

transparent to the program. Unless it specifically requests to be halted a program is unaware of the fact that it does not have the processor all the time.

The state of a program can be changed either by an SVC requesting halting or freeing, or by an interrupt. A second component of the executive is therefore an *interrupt handler*. This activates the appropriate interrupt routine and then changes the state of the program affected, and activates the scheduler. To this end it maintains a *device table* which, for each active device, points to the program control block of the program that is currently waiting on that device. The data structures of the executive are shown in Fig. 2.2.

Allocation of the processor involves dumping the registers and program status word of the current program in its control block, and reloading them from the control block of the program to be restarted. This is known as a *context switch*. The change from program a to program b in fact involves two context switches:

program a ➤ executive
executive ➤ program b

To reduce the overheads of context swtiching, some machines (e.g. the larger PDP11 models) provide a separate set of registers for the executive to use.

We have tacitly assumed that the scheduler will always find a program free to run. If no such program can be found the scheduler must keep scanning the chain until (as a result of an interrupt) a program is freed.

program control blocks

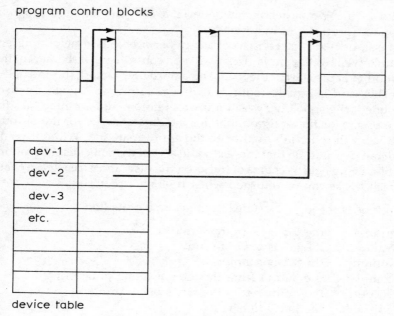

device table

Fig. 2.2   Executive data structures.

An alternative technique is to have at lowest priority a program that never halts. This can do something useful, such as testing the processor, or it can be set to do a processor intensive and time-consuming job, such as finding a new largest prime, or enumerating the configurations of Rubik's Cube. Since it has the lowest priority it will only run if everything else is halted.

2.3.2 Structure of the spooling system

A typical spooling system, built on the basis of a multi-programming executive, consists of three concurrent modules:

(1) A *reader* which reads jobs from cards to a file on the disc.
(2) A *writer* which transfers line-images from a disc file to the printer.
(3) A *job supervisor* which calls compilers, initiates and terminates jobs, and performs the job-sequencing operations of a simple operating system.

These modules are run by the multi-programming executive: the priority ordering is reader > writer > job supervisor, reflecting the critical times of the peripheral devices. They are ordinary programs: the only special facility that need be provided is a mechanism to ensure that control returns to the job supervisor whenever a compiler or user program terminates (normally or abnormally).

We assume that a job consists of a deck of cards consisting of program cards followed by data cards. There will be a control card at the start of the job, another at the start of the data, and a third one to mark the end of the job. (This card is strictly redundant, but requiring it is good for user discipline.) The spooling system must therefore maintain three files for each job: one for the program, one for the data and one for the output. The IOCS will route I/O from or to the appropriate file. Without going into detail, we assume that there is some sort of dynamic disc allocation, with files being held as chains of tracks on the disc, and a free-space chain to which tracks can be returned when no longer required.

A job goes through six states in the course of its life:

(1) Input: the job is being read to disc.
(2) Waiting: the job is ready to run.
(3) Running: the job is running.
(4) Completed: the output from the job is waiting to be printed.
(5) Output: the output from the job is being printed.
(6) Finished: the job is finished.

The spooler will maintain a record for each job known to the system that has not reached the 'finished' state containing the following information:

User-id
Status
Pointer to program file
Pointer to data file
Pointer to output file

An array or linked list of these records forms the *job queue*. This queue is an example of a *shared resource* since it is examined and updated by three separate programs. It is necessary to take care to ensure the integrity of such a shared data area, ensuring that one program does not read from it while updating by another program is in progress.

When the reader sees the header card of a new job, it creates a new entry in the job queue. This entry is not deleted until the status 'finished' is reached: this facilitates restart or rerunning of the job in the event of trouble. The action of the spooling system can now be described quite briefly:

Reader:
    repeat
        read header card
        create queue record

```
        set status to 'input'
        read program to file
        read data to file
        create empty file for output
        set status to 'waiting'
      indefinitely
Writer:
      repeat
        find job with staus 'complete'
        print output
        reclaim file space
        delete queue record
      indefinitely
Job supervisor:
      repeat
        find job with staus 'waiting'
        run compiler
        if no errors then run program
        set status 'complete'
      indefinitely
```

The job supervisor runs the compiler and the compiled program as subroutines, so that it regains control on completion. (Abnormal halts will be trapped by executive, which must return control to the job supervisor.) The IOCS diverts input requests to the program or data file as appropriate, and sends output (including compiler listings, etc.) to the output file.

The above description has assumed that all three modules of the spooling system run indefinitely. In practice this will not be the case. Each time the reader initiates a card-read operation it must halt until the interrupt signalling completion of reading the card; similarly, after sending a line to the line-printer the writer must wait for the interrupt announcing completion of the print operation. Synchronization is obtained by using the interrupt as the restart signal for the appropriate program. Other situations to be catered for include:

(1) No cards in the card-reader – reader must halt.
(2) Printer off-line – writer must halt.
(3) No jobs ready to run – job supervisor must halt.
(4) No output to print – writer must halt.
(5) Job queue full – reader must halt.

Whenever a module halts, we have to ensure that it is eventually restarted when the reason for halting has disappeared. The restart reasons corresponding to the above halt reasons are:

(1) Operator loads cards in card-reader.
(2) Operator puts printer on-line.
(3) Input of a job is completed (signalled by the reader).
(4) Running of a job completed (signalled by the job supervisor).
(5) Queue entry deleted (signalled by writer).

The spooling system modules are synchronized using the halt and restart SVCs described earlier. Each module halts itself in appropriate circumstances. The reader sends a restart signal to the job supervisor whenever input of a job is complete, the writer sends a restart to the reader whenever it completes output for a job, and the job supervisor sends a restart signal to the writer whenever a job has been completed. In most cases the signal will be superfluous, since the program being signalled will not have halted. We therefore redefine the restart operation as 'restart specified program if it is halted': in this way the superfluous restart instructions can be ignored.

When we have programs running concurrently there is always a danger of a *deadlock*, i.e. a situation where two programs are halted, each waiting for the other to do something. We must be sure that this cannot happen. The possibility of deadlock arises because the pre-emptive scheduling imposed by the executive means that a program that is not running at the highest priority can be stopped at an arbitrary point without knowing it. Thus a program might be interrupted while in the middle of updating a shared data area; the higher priority program that now starts running may read this data area and thus obtain incorrect information. Specifically, let us consider the interface between the reader and the job supervisor. Suppose that part of the communication between these modules is a count of the number of jobs in the queue. This count will be held in a shared memory area: whenever the reader completes the input of a job it will increment the count, and whenever the job supervisor starts a job from the queue it will decrement the count. If the count reaches zero the job supervisor will halt itself, to be restarted when the reader completes the input of another job. If the count reaches some predetermined limit the reader will halt, to be restarted by the writer when a queue entry has been deleted. In most machines, testing the count will require at least two instructions, one to load the count in a register, and one to do the actual test. It is therefore possible for the following circumstance to arise. At some time, the count is zero. The job supervisor loads the count into a register as a preliminary to testing it, and at this moment executive pre-empts the job supervisor and starts the reader. The latter sees the card just read is 'end of job', so it increments the count, sends a restart signal to the job supervisor, and starts reading the next job. Since the state of the job supervisor is 'free' (it was pre-empted) the restart signal is ignored. In due course executive allocates the processor to the job supervisor: this continues where it left off, finds the count in the register zero, and therefore halts itself, although there is a job waiting to be run.

This is an example of a situation that can occur whenever programs achieve synchronization by sharing memory. In the worst case we can have the so-called *deadly embrace*, where two programs are halted, each waiting for a signal from the other. A solution to the particular situation outlined above is to make a simple alteration to the restart signalling mechanism. We associate with each program an executive flag called 'wake-up'. If a restart signal is sent to a program that is free but not actually running, its wake-up flag is set, and if a program tries to halt itself when the wake-up flag is set, the halt request is ignored and the wake-up flag is reset. Thus in the example above, when the job supervisor attempted to halt itself it would carry on, test the count again, find it non-zero and proceed correctly.

An alternative method is to require all access to shared data areas to be made via the executive. This ensures that access to the shared area will not be interrupted by a rescheduling, since it will be an *indivisible operation*. The disadvantage of this approach is the overhead of the entries to executive.

2.3.3 Multi-stream spooling systems

Although the kind of system just described is often called a batch system, it is really a continuous flow process, and is better described as a *single stream* spooling system, since it processes a single stream of jobs. If there is sufficient memory space available we can provide a second job supervisor so that two parallel streams of jobs can be run. This can be useful as a way of maximizing processor utilization, since if one stream is held up waiting for a peripheral device the other stream can run. More commonly, however, we use a two-stream system to implement some external scheduling strategy, treating the two streams asymmetrically. Thus suppose we use a pre-emptive scheduling algorithm with stream A assigned a higher priority than stream B. The jobs in stream A will clearly progress at the expense of those in stream B. If we place small short jobs (e.g. program development) in stream A while long 'production' jobs go into stream B, the user will see a rapid turn-round on small jobs, and a somewhat slower turn-round on large jobs.

There are many variations of detail in the organization of such a system. One possibility is for the user to specify the class of his job ('large' or 'small') in the job card: this information is transferred to the job queue, and each job supervisor when scanning the queue looks only at those jobs in the appropriate category. An alternative method employed on large machines equipped with more than one card-reader is to replicate the reader and the job queue. Thus reader A reads jobs from card-reader A and feeds job supervisor A via job queue A, while reader B reads jobs from card-reader B and feeds job supervisor B via job queue B. In either case the system must apply some policing to detect the unscrupulous user who submits a large job, falsely representing it to be a small one. It is necessary for the job supervisor to keep a tally of the CPU time used by each job as it runs, and to abort a job that exceeds the limit appropriate to its type. The actual timing is done by executive: as part of the scheduling operation it updates a record of the CPU time used by the program just pre-empted. A similar technique can be employed to impose a limit on the number of lines output by a job: these are counted by the IOCS, which informs the executive when a preset limit has been exceeded.

In a really large installation with multiple printers a separate writer and printer can be associated with each stream. If the card-reader and printer for the 'fast' stream are situated in an area accessible to users we have a so-called *cafeteria* system in which users can submit a card deck and then wait for their output to appear. This same organization also makes it easy to implement a *remote-job-entry* system, in which the card-reader and printer are geographically remote from the computer, being connected by some sort of communication link. (We have glossed over the problem of operator communication for the remote station.)

The hardware of some second-generation machines (notably the IBM System 360) makes it easy to establish partitions of fixed size, and for such a machine the multi-stream spooling system is a natural mode of operation. Indeed, in IBM jargon 'partition' is often used as a synonym for 'job supervisor', since there is a one-to-one correspondence between them. Even with more flexible memory-allocation hardware the multi-stream organization is the easiest to implement, and it was the basis for the successful GEORGE 2 system on ICL machines. However, despite the simplicity of the scheme, it has several major disadvantages. The most significant of these is that the only priority ordering is between streams: within one stream the jobs are executed in a strict first-in first-out sequence. This may suffice in some user environments, but a more elaborate scheduling philosophy may be desirable. For example, in a system with many competing users there may be good reason to order the jobs in a way that takes account of the resources (budget) available to the user, and his past usage of the system. We may also wish to vary priorities in response to the length of time a job has been waiting, or in response to a request from the system manager. To achieve these ends it is necessary to replace the multiple job supervisors, each running jobs from a separate stream, by a single job supervisor that is capable of multi-programming several jobs. The supervisor selects the jobs to be multi-programmed according to some externally defined scheduling strategy, and hence has the flexibility to meet the special requirements outlined above. This kind of working is relatively easy to organize in a machine that has memory mapping hardware (which facilitates the division of the memory into a variable number of partitions of varying size, in a manner that will be described later), and is basically the way of working adopted for the highly successful GEORGE 3 system on the larger third-generation ICL machines. It is much more difficult on machines without memory mapping, but it can still be managed: OS/MVT on the IBM 360s is the classic example. (The acronym MVT stands for 'Multi-programming with a Variable number of Tasks', but is widely believed to mean 'Multi-programming with a Vast amount of Trouble'.)

This mode of working introduces a new component of the operating system, the High Level Scheduler (HLS). The function of the HLS is to decide which jobs are to be multi-programmed by the job supervisor. Each time a job finishes the job supervisor calls the HLS. The HLS first decides whether another job should be started, and if the answer is yes it chooses the job from amongst those marked 'waiting' in the input queue, loads the program and informs executive that this program is to be run. The HLS should not be confused with the low-level scheduler in the executive, which actually shares the processor between the operating system modules and the jobs being multi-programmed.

The precise working of the HLS depends on the management strategy adopted by the installation. The aim is to order the jobs in the queue by assigning a figure of merit or priority to them: this will determine the choice of job to be started. Typically the user will provide estimates of CPU usage, memory requirements, etc., or he may be required to assign his job to one of a number of predefined classes. This information will be used by the HLS to determine an *a priori* priority for the job. The HLS may also have access to information about the user's allocation of resources, the amount of his allocation still unused, and his current rate of use. This can be used to influence the *a priori* priority.

It is important to ensure that all jobs get done eventually, even if preference is given to jobs of certain kinds. For example, if short jobs are given priority it is necessary to ensure that a long job does not languish in the queue indefinitely. One technique is to tag each job with its time of arrival (a *time stamp*), so that long-waiting jobs can be spotted. Another technique is to increment the priority of jobs in the queue at regular intervals. In this way the natural passage of time will ensure that an unpopular job finally acquires enough priority to beat anything else in the queue, so that all jobs get done eventually. (It is important to appreciate that this increase in priority only affects the actions of the high-level scheduler in selecting a job to be run. Once selected, a user job is assigned a priority by the low-level scheduler that is independent of its previous priority, and depends only on its class.) It is also important to be able to guarantee that jobs will be done in a certain sequence. (For example, if program A produces data to be used by program B there is no point in a clever scheduling algorithm deciding to do B first.)

The *a priori* priority is not the only factor that decides whether a job should be run: account must also be taken of the availability of sufficient memory and other resource requirements. For example, if an installation has only four tape transports, there is no point in trying to run two jobs which between them need five transports. The design of the HLS must take account of this and other allocation problems; we return to this point later.

The executive for such a system is broadly similar to that for simpler systems. The main difference is that it has to deal with a varying number of programs. This obviously affects the low-level scheduler, and also introduces an entirely new executive function, memory management. When the HLS selects a candidate job to run, it must acquire a suitable memory 'slot' from executive; conversely, when a job is finished the memory slot occupied by its program can be made available for reallocation by executive. The executive therefore has to keep track of empty slots in memory, and to allocate these in response to requests from the HLS. The precise way in which this can be done is discussed in a later chapter.

Adapting the multi-programming executive to deal with a variable number of programs is trivial, given the chained structure of program control blocks. A more substantial problem arises from the fact that we can no longer assign a fixed priority ordering to all the programs being multi-programmed, since the readers and writers must take precedence over the user programs, but all the user programs are of essentially the same priority. One solution is as follows. The program control blocks for the system programs are placed on the chain in order of priority, as before, and are followed by a block which points to a circular chain of program control blocks for user programs. The scheduler is entered whenever the status of a program changes, or when the clock interrupt is generated. Its action can be described as follows:

if there is a system program free
then run it (choosing the one of highest priority that is free)
else if not clock interrupt
then carry on running the current users program if it is free
else run the next user program in the circular chain.

Thus system programs still enjoy pre-emptive scheduling, but user programs are run on a round-robin basis, with a fixed time quantum determined by the clock interrupt rate.

An alternative design is as follows. We add an additional field to the program control block, in which we accumulate the CPU time used by the program. At regular intervals the chain of program control blocks is scanned and reordered so that the program control blocks occur in increasing order of CPU time used. The accumulated total is then set to zero in all the program control blocks. The effect of this is that peripheral-limited programs (such as the readers and writers) which use little CPU time always stay near the head of the queue while processor-intensive programs migrate towards the end of the queue. The system is self-regulating. As programs change from being processor-intensive to being peripheral bound they will move up the queue: likewise a program near the head of the priority queue that suddenly becomes processor-intensive will rapidly lose priority and so will not be allowed to monopolize the processor.

Finally, we note that this kind of spooling system can readily be extended to cope with a diversity of output devices. The job table maintained by the spooling system is amended to keep a record of the type of device for which each output file is intended, and instead of a single writer, we have one for each peripheral. These scan the table looking for a complete file destined for their type of device, and halt themselves if no such file exists. Each time the job supervisor finishes a job it sends a restart signal to *all* the writers so as to avoid a deadlock situation. Multiple readers are easily taken into account, and remote-job-entry (RJE) stations are trivially accommodated. When the reader for an RJE station creates a new entry in the queue, it sets the output device to be the associated printer, so that in due course the RJE writer will find the output file and print it.

2.4   TIME-SHARING AND MULTI-ACCESS SYSTEMS

Although the development of spooling systems improved the overall throughput of the computing system, it interposed a barrier between the system and the user, who no longer had the benefit of 'hands-on' working, with its associated possibility of immediate interaction with the program. There was thus an incentive to develop systems in which the convenience of hands-on operation could be combined with the efficiency of a fully-utilized processor. This led someone to have an idea of startling simplicity, a variation on the idea of multi-programming that was at the basis of the spooling systems then in use. If a number of programs could be allowed to use the processor in strict sequence, each having possession for a small time-slice (or quantum), then if the time-slice was small enough all the programs would appear to progress in parallel. If each program was associated with a user at a terminal (in those days a Teletype), each user would have hands-on access (on-line access in modern terminology) and would have the impression of using his own personal computing system.

Since there is unlikely to be room in the memory for all the programs simultaneously, we allocate a number of 'slots' on the disc, each able to hold a *core-image*, i.e. a snapshot dump of memory and register contents. (The name core-image derives from the time when core storage was the usual form of memory. The usage persists although core storage is rarely used in modern machines.) A clock interrupt provides a timing mechanism, and at the end of a time-slice the core image of the current program is *rolled-out* to its place on the disc, and the next core-image is *rolled-in* (a process known as *swapping*). In addition, the user is provided with a *filing system* that allows him to store and retrieve program and data files identified by symbolic names, without having to worry about the details of how they are stored on disc. An interactive file-editor, driven from the terminal, completes the system.

In practice, things are not quite so simple. If the user is to have the impression of having hands-on access to a machine, it is essential that input from the keyboard should always be accepted, and it is similarly desirable that the flow of output to the terminal should not be erratic. It is therefore essential that I/O should proceed whether the program is currently running or not. The problem is easily solved by the provision of buffers for input and output. Characters from the keyboard are accumulated a line at a time in the input buffer, and when the program calls for input it is halted only if the buffer is empty. Similarly, output is accumulated in a buffer, the program halting if the buffer is full. The system sends output from the buffer to the terminal as long as there is anything in the buffer, independently of the program state. The scheduling algorithm is thus as follows:

Run the current program until:

either the time quantum expires
or it calls for input and the buffer is empty
or it calls for output and the buffer is full
then run the next program in the round-robin sequence that is not held up waiting for input or output.

The system is elegantly self-regulating. A program that produces a sudden burst of output will fill the buffer and halt: in due course the buffer will empty and the program will proceed, without the user being aware of any break in the smooth flow of his output. If the input buffer is a single line, the user will be instructed not to type until he receives a prompt for the next line. However, many systems provide a multi-line input buffer which allows the user the facility of *type-ahead*.

A variation on the simple round-robin scheduling is to introduce an element of pre-emptive scheduling. In this version a program that is waiting for input or output is skipped by the scheduling algorithm until it becomes free: it then goes to the head of the queue and is given the next available time-slice. This type of scheduling increases the apparent responsiveness of a program to what is happening at the terminal, and is a good example of 'human engineering'.

A time-sharing system such as the one we have described is still inefficient in processor utilization since its performance is dominated by the time taken in swapping, during which no programs are actually progressing. (For this reason one of the earliest of such systems had special hardware that allowed one core-image to be written to the drum while another core image was being read. These actions were strictly synchronized so that the writing of a word to the drum was immediately followed by the reading of a replacement word.) On the other hand, the strategy is very easy to implement, and the virtues of being able to implement a system quickly should not be underestimated. There are many examples of simple software systems running and making money, while more elaborate and sophisticated systems are struggling in the pangs of development.

The swapping overhead is made even worse if a program halts for I/O soon after being swapped in. If the memory is sufficiently large the situation can be alleviated by *anticipatory swapping*. Thus suppose there is room in memory for three programs simultaneously (i.e. three partitions), then we aim to keep in memory not only the current program but also the next two in the round-robin. When the current program finishes or halts, or the time quantum expires, the next program is already in memory, and only requires a context switch (i.e. loading of registers) before it can proceed. The swapping out of the previous program, and the swapping in of the next in sequence is thus overlapped with the running of the current program, and in theory swapping overheads are reduced to zero. This ideal is rarely achieved, but a substantial decrease in the overhead is possible. The scheduler will of course skip over a program that is in fact waiting for I/O when its turn to be swapped arrives.

We have so far concentrated on the mechanics of running several users' programs simultaneously, and dealing with their input and output. A user will generally want to run several programs in the course of an on-line session (editor, compiler, compiled program, debugger, editor . . .), and must be provided with a means of controlling all this activity.

This is the role of the *command interpreter*, which reads commands from the keyboard and loads the appropriate utility or user programs. There is a copy of the command interpreter in every user's core-image: it is the on-line equivalent of the job supervisor. With one exception, the command interpreter has no special privileges, and runs as an ordinary program. The one exception is that if a program stops or comes to an untimely end, executive must return control to the appropriate command interpreter.

The early time-sharing systems were dedicated systems, often running on a minicomputer. Their success led to a demand for time-sharing to be incorporated with 'batch' computing on large mainframes. This was conveniently achieved by packaging the time-sharing system as a subsystem which appeared as a single 'job' to the main operating system. With such a set-up we have to provide two-level scheduling: the executive allocates a certain proportion of the CPU time to the subsystem, which in turn allocates its share of the CPU to the time-sharing users on a round-robin basis.

A superficially attractive idea is to combine time-sharing facilities with a multi-programming spooling system by adding a number of 'on-line' jobs, each associated with a remote terminal, to the jobs controlled by the multi-programming supervisor. The on-line jobs are given high priority by the High Level Scheduler so that the users get a good response. This was the underlaying concept of the ICL GEORGE 3 system. Unfortunately, it was not possible on the available hardware to keep a lot of 'on-line' jobs simultaneously in memory, and the overheads of organizing the swapping in and out while still running the batch work were such that this elegant idea was never as successful in practice as had been hoped.

2.4.1 Classification of multi-access systems

Multi-access systems can be classified in various ways, according to different criteria. Two classifications are particularly useful, one based on generality, the other based on interactive capabilities. On the first criterion we can distinguish three classes of system:

(1) Dedicated systems: these systems offer only one programming language, most commonly BASIC, sometimes APL. There are numerous commercially available systems of this kind.
(2) Multi-language systems: these provide compilers or interpreters for a number of languages sharing a common filing and editing system. Typical of this class is the DEC RSTS/E system. At one time it was

common to include a 'desk-calculator' language, but this is less common nowadays.

(3) General-purpose systems: the major characteristic of this kind of system is that it is extensible. It is possible for the user at his terminal to define new commands and introduce new compilers. Systems of this sort generally provide facilitites for sharing files, so that work done by one user can be made available to the wider community of users. The multi-access facilities of this kind of system are often combined with conventional 'batch' facilities. Programs running in batch mode have access to the filing system, and a job can therefore be run in whichever mode suits its particular state of development. The ability to introduce jobs into the batch stream from a terminal, known as *conversational remote job entry* is particularly useful. The first example of such a general-purpose system was the classic CTSS (compatible time sharing system) developed at MIT.

Alternatively, we can classify systems according to their interactive capabilities. At one extreme there can be full interaction, with a program able to initiate terminal I/O at any stage. At the other extreme is the type of system in which such interaction is restricted to the operating system programs: once a user program is started it is cut off from the terminal until it reaches a successful or unsuccessful end. This type of restriction is usually imposed in mainframe systems where the time-sharing system co-exists with a heavy batch-processing load. Full interaction involves programs spending long times waiting for input and output, and this can impose an unacceptable load on such a system. Overall throughput is improved by limiting the availability of interactive facilities. However, minicomputer-based time-sharing systems being designed as multi-user systems, and having little if any batch load, give the user the full benefits of interactive working.

2.5 TRANSACTION PROCESSING SYSTEMS

These have already been alluded to briefly. In such a system a large number of terminals are on-line to a single program and associated database (e.g. an airline reservation system). Each terminal can request an operation chosen from a small repertoire of services, e.g. make a reservation, cancel a reservation, display available flights, etc. Each such exchange with the program is called a *transaction*, hence the generic name of this kind of system. The heart of the system is the *dispatcher* which polls the terminals in regular sequence to see if they require service. If a terminal is found with a request pending the system reads the message from the terminal, loads the module that deals with this kind of request and starts it. The module may return to the dispatcher if it requires to conduct an exchange with the terminal, or it may call another module to continue the processing. Large-scale TP systems (e.g. airline reservation systems) run in dedicated machines, but as with time-sharing systems it is possible to run a TP system as a subsystem along with a batch-processing load. However, it is difficult to guarantee response times in such an environment, and such combined systems have not in general been outstandingly successful.

2.6. MICROCOMPUTER MONITOR SYSTEMS

We now come to recent history. The early microcomputers used paper tape (or possible cassette tape) for auxiliary storage, and did not have anything remotely resembling an operating system, being driven manually from the keyboard with at most some programs in ROM to read and write cassette tapes. The advent of floppy-disc-based systems brought with it the need for software to exploit the disc, and the concept of the 'disc operating system' (or DOS) was borrowed from the minicomputer world. Basically, all that a disc-operating system does is to provide a method of storing programs and data in *files* on the disc, and a mechanism whereby files can be retrieved and programs run in response to simple commands from the keyboard. A number of such systems were developed; one of them, CP/M, became a *de facto* standard for 8-bit machines using the Z80 or 8080 CPU chip, and the remainder of this section is based on CP/M as an example.

CP/M is made up of three modules, called BDOS, BIOS and CCP.

(1) BDOS, the Basic Disc Operating System, is the heart of CP/M. It allows the user to see the floppy disc as a number of *files* of varying length, identified by symbolic names. BDOS performs dynamic allocation of disc sectors so that when a file is deleted the space that it occupied can be reused. BDOS also provides a hardware-independent I/O interface to a console devise (usually a VDU), a 'list' device (usually a printer) and to two further character devices called, for historical (paper tape) reasons, 'reader' and 'punch'. These devices form a pair, one input device and one output device, and can be used to access a cassette tape or a telephone modem, for example.

(2) CCP (Command Control Processor) is responsible for the user interface. CCP operates in an endless loop, reading a command from the keyboard, obeying it, then returning to the start to read another command. A few simple commands are implemented by code within CCP itself, but for the most part command programs are stored as files, and CCP obeys a command by reading the appropriate file into

the *transient program area* (TPA) and executing the program so loaded. All command programs terminate by re-entering CCP. Commands provided in this way include a context editor (ED), an assembler (ASM), and a peripheral interchange program (PIP).

(3) BIOS (Basic Input Output System) is the only part of CP/M that is hardware-dependent. It implements the system calls of BDOS, mapping the hardware-independent interface on to the actual hardware devices in use. Each microcomputer manufacturer supporting CP/M provides a BIOS customized to his particular hardware.

The interface provided by BDOS is implemented as a set of *system calls* that can be used by any program, not only the CCP. These system calls provide a uniform *software interface* for programs, and it is this aspect of CP/M that has been largely responsible for its popularity, since it makes application software portable over a wide range of hardware.

CP/M is a relatively unsophisticated system. The 8080 and Z80 have no memory protection facilities; CP/M divides the memory into four partitions, which are enforced purely by user discipline (see Fig. 2.3).

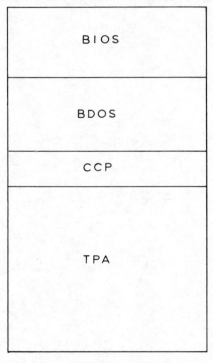

Fig. 2.3 CP/M memory allocation.

CP/M is a strictly sequential system: there is no overlapping of input–output, and once a program requests an I/O transfer it loses control of the processor until such time as the transfer is complete. In the early versions of the system the repertoire of commands was restricted by the limited number of files available (an upper limit of 64). However, later versions of the system are able to handle large-capacity 'Winchester' discs, thus removing this restriction. The structure of CP/M is discussed in more detail in later chapters.

3
Operating system architecture

3.1 THE NEED FOR CONCURRENCY

In the preceding chapter we have followed the historical development of operating systems. As more complicated systems were developed, designers gained an understanding of some of the fundamental principles underlying operating system design, and, in contrast to the *ad hoc* basis of earlier systems, modern systems are gradually coming to be founded on clear architectural principles (though these tend to be hidden under a mass of superficial detail in many cases!).

CP/M is a fundamentally simple operating system because it is strictly sequential. Control moves between the various modules in response to user commands or system calls from programs, but at any one time only one module of CP/M is active. When the user types a command, CCP passes control to BDOS to read the command file into the TPA and BDOS then hands control to the command program. This in turn may call BDOS or BIOS, and will eventually return control to CCP. This linear sequencing is simple but restrictive, and even in a 'personal' computer system we may want something more. For example, if our system includes a printer we will not wish to wait for a long file to be printed; we would prefer to get on with something else (e.g. a compilation) while the printing is in progress. This particular problem can be solved by the use of one of the hardware 'printer spoolers' that are on the market, which provide a large RAM buffer that can be filled rapidly by the CPU, and emptied at leisure by the printer. But there are other situations in which we may want to do more than one thing at once. For example, we might want to get on with some editing while a long compilation is in progress, or we might wish to suspend an edit while we run a program to generate data to be included in the file being edited. For these reasons the latest personal computer operating systems (e.g. Concurrent CP/M-86) provide a capability for multiple concurrent tasks.

In a larger system there will be two further levels of concurrency in addition to concurrency at the user level. There will be a requirement for concurrent system activity (e.g. anticipatory swapping in a time-sharing system), and for concurrency between multiple simultaneous users. Concurrent operation is thus essential for anything but the simplest system, and is characteristic of almost all operating systems.

In the historical development, such concurrency was seen in the context of sequential programs, and a variety of special mechanisms were introduced to cope with it. The essential and central feature of modern operating system architecture is that we abandon the purely serial concept, and regard concurrent operation as the norm. Thus we view the operating system as a number of concurrent activities which run largely independently of each other, but from time to time exchange messages or signals. We describe such a collection of activities as *loosely coupled*. Of course, this structure has to be implemented on a machine which is not inherently capable of such simultaneous operation, since it probably has only one processor. We thus divide the operating system into a *super-structure*, which is a collection of concurrent activities, and a *kernel* whose function is to provide an environment of apparent concurrency. The activities run in a quasi-parallel mode, since the number of activities genuinely running simultaneously is limited by the hardware to one, or perhaps two in some cases. The kernel shares the physical resources (memory and processor(s)) between the superstructure activities and administers communication between, and synchronization of, those activities.

Contrary to first fears, treating parallelism as the natural state makes the description of the system simpler. All the problems of parallel or quasi-parallel running are encapsulated in the kernel, and the design of the rest of the system can be completed without any concern for the mechanics of concurrent operation. Moreover, it becomes trivially easy to deal with multi-processor systems, since only the kernel needs to know how many processors actually exist. Within the kernel the multi-processor system is treated as the norm, with the single processor as a (very common) degenerate case.

3.2   THE PROCESS CONCEPT

An activity comprises a series of actions devoted to achieving some well-defined end, e.g. the transfer of a block of data from a device, the compiling of a source program, etc. This will be effected by the execution of one or more programs in association with some data. We described the dynamic invocation of a program as a *process*. A process is essentially different from a program. A process is dynamic, while a program is static; moreover, a process may involve the execution of several different programs, while conversely a particular program may at one time be part of several processes. Indeed, a process may not be associated with a program at all – it may be a function carried out entirely by the hardware. Thus on this definition an autonomous I/O channel may be regarded as a process while it is executing channel commands.

In an ideal system there would be no need to distinguish processes from activities: the two would be identical. In practice we do not have an unlimited supply of processors and memory, and so we must separate the abstract concept of an activity from its realization as a process. An activity can be either *active* or *halted*: active if it is 'running' and halted if it is waiting for an event or a signal from another activity. Its realization as a process has three states, *running*, *free* and *halted*. A running process is one that is actually executing on a processor: a free process is one that is able to run if a processor was available to run it, and a halted process corresponds exactly to a halted activity. Thus we conceive of the operating system as a collection of activities, implemented as processes. An important feature of this approach is that there is a simple correspondence between the natural modules of the operating system and the activities (processes) that make up its implementation.

3.2.1 An historical note

The concept of process introduced here as the central concept underlying operating system structure is usually believed to have originated in the Multics system, developed in the USA in the mid-sixties. In fact, the fundamental idea of organizing concurrent activities in this way originated earlier in the Atlas Supervisor, where what we now call a process was called (for irrelevant historical reasons) an SER. The main functions of the kernel were carried out by a routine called the *co-ordinator*. As is to be expected with the first implementation of a novel idea, there were many *ad hoc* features, and the system lacked a modular structure: none the less it should be given due credit. The Atlas Supervisor introduced many innovative ideas: the pity is that they got submerged, and had to be rediscovered, with much trouble, nearly a decade later.

3.3 PROCESSES AND PROCESS STRUCTURE

From now on we shall follow the usual convention and refer to processes rather than activities. A running process involves a program, some data, and a processor to run it. It is convenient to define the *process image* to be the collection of program code, data and instantaneous processor state (register contents, processor status word, etc.). A process that is free or halted is represented by its 'frozen' process image; a running process is an association of a process image and a processor.

Some of the processes that make up an operating system exist all the time that the system is running. Others have a more restricted existence: they are created, and having performed their appointed task they die. An important characteristic is that processes interact, in the sense that the completion of any one process may be dependent on the operation of one or more other processes. This interaction may take the form of an exchange of signals, e.g. an I/O process signalling to a computing process that the transfer of some data has been completed, or it may take the form of more elaborate communication by means of shared data areas. Operating systems are generally built round a philosophy of one or other of these varieties of interaction. If all inter-process communication is by means of messages, the kernel acts as a kind of 'telephone exchange' in addition to its other functions. This kind of architecture is particularly well suited to distributed computing systems, since provided there is a well-defined interface for an inter-process message channel, it is possible to establish co-operation between processes running in different physical machines.

In the course of its operation, a process can invoke other processes in various ways. Important amongst these are:

(1) Initiating another process to run in parallel with the parent process.
(2) Initiating another process and then waiting for that process to finish.
(3) Transfer of control in linear sequence to another process, i.e. initiating another process and then committing suicide.

In cases (1) and (2) there is likely to be communication between the parent process and its offspring. In the case of parallel running, each may inform the other of its progress. In case (2), the 'child' process will send a signal on completion to 'wake up' its parent, and may wish to report on the outcome of its activity (e.g. successful or unsuccessful conclusion). A particular case of signalling is the 'supervised' process. During its operation a process may generate various 'contingencies', e.g. attempt to access memory outside its partition, attempt to write to a read-only file, etc. A process may choose to field these events and deal with them as they arise; alternatively it may be specified that such contingencies are to be notified to the parent process, the child process being halted meanwhile. This sort of structure allows the vetting of privileged operations requested by an unprivileged process. Communication between processes is simplified if they are arranged in a strict hierarchy in which any process (apart from a primeval 'root' process) has a unique 'parent'. Such a hierarchy is particularly useful in resolving problems that arise if a process terminates prematurely; when a process dies or is killed, all its subordinate processes die with it. The hierarchy also provides for supervision of subordinate processes, and facilitates resource allocation in a systematic way.

The process concept provides a very effective way of structuring the concurrent activities within an operating system. There is, however, a class of system activity that does not fit conveniently into the process model. Processes need to call on the system for various services, e.g. opening a file, checking the status of a device, requesting more memory space, etc. There is no point in providing such services on a concurrent basis, since the requesting process cannot proceed until the request has been serviced. These services are provided by a set of *system calls*; these are SVCs that appear as procedure calls into the kernel, with a normal procedure exit when the necessary action has been completed. Although the system call appears to the user to be executed 'in-line', in fact there will at some point in the system call be a switch of environments, since system processes usually have a private stack. The system call can be described as a separate phase of the user process, since the two never execute concurrently. This kind of change within a process does not have the overheads of a complete context switch.

3.4   FUNCTIONS OF THE KERNEL

The kernel has a two-fold role: it simulates concurrent activity for the superstructure processes, and it also provides the interface with the hardware, receiving all signals from the outside world. Its simulation of parallel activity is a direct extension of the multi-programming executive concept developed in Chapter 2. The kernel maintains a list of current processes, keeps track of those that are free to proceed, and shares the processor(s) between them according to a chosen strategy implemented by a *scheduler* that is entered whenever any process changes its status. The kernel also administers the storage allocation strategy. An essential part of the kernel is the mechanism whereby processes are created: it also administers the synchronization of processes and the passing of messages between them.

Processor and memory allocation are examples of a general function of the kernel, *resource allocation*. It is also responsible for the control of *resource sharing*. For example, processes are usually written so that the program code is not self-modifying. Such *re-entrant* code is shareable, and the kernel oversees the sharing.

3.5   OPERATING SYSTEM STRUCTURES

The operating system can be split into a kernel and a superstructure. It is often convenient to partition the superstructure into a number of subsystems – one or more 'batch stream' supervisors with associated spooling systems; a file-system manager; a multi-access supervisor; a transaction-processing supervisor, and so on. These are to be regarded as running concurrently, and each subsystem will be made up of components that run concurrently (cf. the description of the spooling system in Chapter 2.)

Within this general framework, two broad strategies of system design can be discerned. In the most general strategy, every distinguishable system activity is made into a process. Thus a user job (i.e. unit of work) will consist of a number of processes activated in linear sequence, or may involve processes that run concurrently. In the most general case the command interpreter runs as a process, and for each command obeyed (edit, compile, etc.) a separate process is created. The command interpreter will usually wait for the process so created to terminate, but the possibility is open for the two to run in parallel, facilitating the creation of 'background' jobs. Indeed, as an extreme case it may be possible to have two command interpreters running in parallel.

This structure for the operating system offers great flexibility, but can have some disadvantages. The most serious potential disadvantage is that since each request for system activity involves activating another process, the overheads of process management may become excessive. (Activating a new process involves saving the processor state of the current process and loading the registers for the new process – the so-called *context switch*. If the new process is not already in memory there will be further overheads in finding a suitable space and loading the new process-image.) Thus a process-based architecture must be used with discretion. Processes should correspond to recognizably distinct and potentially concurrent activities, e.g. disc transfers. System activity that is by its nature sequential should be implemented in-process. For more substantial (but still sequential) activities it may still be possible to avoid a context switch. In many process-based architectures a process has associated with it three *segments* in memory: its code, its stack and its data. When 'linear' system activity is requested the code and data segments are exchanged for those of the system activity. Thus the same *process* is running, but with a different *program*. (It is the stack that gives a definable separate identity to a process, since a separate stack is an essential requirement for parallel execution.) A further possible disadvantage of a process-based architecture arises from the nature of inter-process communication. If for example a process requires a disc transfer, it will enter a request in a shared data area prior to activating the process responsible for disc transfers. Thus all requests for disc activity are serialized, although some degree of parallel processing might have been possible.

3.5.1. 'In-process' architecture

UNIX is a good example of a process-structured operating system. A very different strategy is used in ICL's VME. Here the process concept is used only to achieve concurrency *between* users (and to a lesser extent concurrency of system activity). There is no concurrency at the individual user level, and with a few small exceptions *all* system activity is carried out in-process, hence the description of the system as an 'in-process architecture'. A process is associated with each user, and the code for *all* system activity appears simultaneously in the process images of *all user processes*. System activity is carried out by procedure calls within a single process image. Since the system code appears in all process images, systems activities are shared, avoiding the enforced serialization noted earlier, and avoiding the expense of context switching for every user activity. At first sight it might appear dangerous to have an operating system activity appearing in more than one process image. In fact it is quite safe. As we shall see in the next chapter, there is only one physical copy of the code and data: the sharing is a piece of electronic sleight of hand. If two process images share the same data area, there is no trouble unless one writes at the same time as the other reads the segment. Thus we need protection only when data areas are written, and we shall see later how this can be enforced.

3.5.2 Virtual machines

In VME *all* the code required for a job (user code, superstructure, supervisory code *and* kernel code) is placed in the single process image. Each job now consists of a conglomeration of precedures that call each other in arbitrarily complicated ways, but run in a strictly serial manner as a single process. Since each process is allocated a subset of the machine's total resources (memory, disc space, peripherals etc.) it forms a *virtual machine* (VM), and the job of the kernel is to share resources between a number of VMs so that they appear to progress in parallel. When a user job genuinely needs concurrent activity (e.g. for input/output spooling), this is effected by calling on an *out-of-process subsystem* that runs in a separate VM (i.e. as a separate process).

This concept of the virtual machine has a number of apparent advantages. For example, a multi-user system such as a time-sharing system can be produced by constructing a single-user terminal system running in its own VM, and then replicating it as many times as required. Similarly, a transaction-processing system can run as a subsystem in its own VM. Unfortunately, this can be a naïve view if the overhead of switching between VMs is not taken into account. The response-time required by terminals dictates a scheduling strategy that runs each VM for a short time-quantum. The consequent context switches can be crippling, making the system unacceptably slow, if great care has not been taken to optimize the context switch. A further and more substantial disadvantage of the full-blooded in-process architecture used in VME is that it completely rules out the possibility of a user job having parallel activity within itself. The traditional view of computing with mainframes is that this is not an important requirement anyway, but it is becoming apparent from UNIX and similar systems (e.g. Concurrent CP/M-86) that concurrent activity at the user level can yield unexpected benefits.

3.5.3   Virtual machines in IBM systems

The virtual machine architecture of VME as just described should not be confused with the similarly named IBM operating system concept exemplified by the VM/370 (Virtual Machine 370) system. In the IBM system the VMs are faithful replicas of the physical 370, right down to I/O channel commands and privileged instructions. The motivation of the IBM system was to allow an installation to run two different (IBM) operating systems simultaneously, by loading them into different VMs. In addition a terminal system, CMS, was provided which used the technique described above of replicating a single-user system. The original VM/370 was an elegant concept, but suffered severe penalties in efficiency. For example, memory allocation tended to be done twice over, once by the operating system running in a VM, and once by the virtual machine mechanism. Later versions have improved the efficiency by hardware enhancements, though at the expense of losing some of the conceptual elegance of the system.

3.6   INTERRUPTS

The generalized process architecture removes the artificial asymmetry inherent in the classic interrupt system. If one process (e.g. an I/O channel) is producing information and another process is consuming it, there is complete symmetry – the producer cannot proceed if the consumer does not take the information, and the consumer cannot proceed if the producer does not produce information. We thus have two co-operating processes that need to communicate and maintain synchronization; the interrupt is nothing more that a crude inter-process message. Besides being used to synchronize peripheral transfers, in most computer systems interrupts are also used to signal various contingencies such as address violations, overflow, etc. In a process architecture one could use these interrupts as a signal to halt the current process and activate another process to deal with the contingency. This is not a good idea – apart from the overheads of context switching, many of the contingencies need to be analysed in the context in which they occurred. The interrupt thus acts as a forced entry to a procedure provided by the system (or possibly by the user) which deals with the particular contingency in-process.

The details of interrupt handling depend on the particular hardware organization. Typically, control goes to a location determined by the nature of the interrupt (a 'vectored interrupt'), and the processor state is changed from 'normal' to 'system'. On some machines (e.g. the larger PDP11s) there is also a switch to a different register set and stack, i.e. a hardware-implemented context switch. Initial processing of the interrupt is the province of a part of the kernel called the *interrupt handler*. This will perform a minimal context switch if the hardware has not already done so: subsequent action depends on the nature of the interrupt. There are four possibilities.

(1) The interrupt is anticipated, i.e. it is a result of an earlier action by a process, which is waiting for it. The interrupt handler generates the appropriate signal to the waiting process and passes control to the scheduler.
(2) The interrupt, which may or may not be anticipated, involves only 'housekeeping', e.g. incrementing a block count on a peripheral transfer. The interrupt routine does the housekeeping then resumes the interrupted process.
(3) The interrupt requires substantial activity (e.g. a system call requesting disc transfers). A process is created and added to the scheduler's list: the scheduler is then entered.
(4) The interrupt arises from a contingency e.g. overflow. An appropriate kernel procedure is called; this may cause a new process to be created if necessary.

4
Processes and virtual machines

4.1 INTRODUCTION

In this chapter we look in some detail at the structure of the kernel. As we have seen, the kernel is a direct descendant of the multi-programming executive. Its role is to provide an abstract-machine interface at which multiple processes can co-exist and run concurrently. It handles process creation and deletion, and process synchronization and communication. A particular case of this latter is the handling of interrupts. The kernel handles *all* interaction with the raw hardware, so that even operating system processes see an abstract machine that is more amenable than the real machine. (The whole process of operating system development can be seen as the successive definition of abstract machines, each based on its predecessor, which provide interfaces suited to the particular level of operation.) The main difference between the multi-programming executive and the kernel is that the latter deals with a larger number of processes, in a dynamic situation where processes are created and deleted in an unpredictable manner.

4.2 SCHEDULING

The first function of the kernel is to share the available processors between the processes that are able to run. In general there will be a number of active processes, m say, and a smaller number, n, of processors. (Usually, $n = 1$.) The processors must be allocated in such a way as to satisfy an overall scheduling policy. This may specify, for example, that all processes are to progress together as far as they are able, or it may specify some priority ordering among the processes. The pool of potentially active processes is usually quite large, and it is sometimes convenient to have a separate level of scheduling outside the kernel to select a subset of the potentially active processes to be run in quasi-parallel mode by the kernel. This external scheduling mechanism may also assign or change priorities, but all this is transparent to the kernel.

For the moment we restrict ourselves to the *low-level scheduler* which implements the apparent concurrent running of a set of processes.

Each process is represented by a *process-descriptor*, which contains *inter alia*:

Process-id: a unique identifier allocated at process creation.

State: can be 'running', 'free', or 'halted'.

Memory location: records the position of the process image in memory.

Scheduling information: (e.g. priority).

The process image typically consists of a code segment, a data segment, a stack segment and a system data segment (containing contents of CPU registers, descriptors for open files, etc.). Thus the 'memory location' field in the process descriptor may in fact contain a number of pointers. Allocation of a single processor is now just a matter of selecting one of the free processes to be run. A simple approach is to chain together the descriptors of all processes known to the system, and to scan this chain to find a free process. In practice we usually keep free and halted processes on different chains so as to minimize the scanning to be done by the scheduler.

The macroscopic scheduling philosophy is achieved by specifying on what occasions the chain is to be scanned to reallocate the processor, and the algorithm to be used to choose one process to be run. Three simple strategies are:

(1) 'Run-to-completion': the process descriptor chain is ordered according to externally specified priorities. Whenever the current process halts (either because it has finished or because it is unable for the time being to proceed) the chain is scanned from the start.
(2) Pre-emptive priority scheduling: as (1), except that the chain is scanned whenever the status of *any* process changes in response to a signal from itself or from another process.
(3) 'Round-robin': the ordering of the chain is not significant. It is scanned in a cyclic manner, starting from the current process, whenever the current process terminates or is unable to proceed, and whenever the interval timer generates an interrupt.

Case (1) was the strategy adopted by the pioneering Atlas Supervisor. Although described as 'run-to-completion', there is an important qualification that once a process has halted because it cannot proceed, there may be an arbitrarily long wait before the processor is next allocated to it, even though the process may in the meantime have been freed by another process. Thus this strategy does not allow of processes with critical response times such as arise in the control of some peripheral devices. The original Atlas implementation allowed a short sequence of code (about 20 instructions) to be obeyed after an interrrupt before the associated process was marked as free. With careful attention to programming, this alleviated the problem of critical response times (since none of the devices were particularly fast by present-day standards). A further technique used was to include voluntary 'halt-points' in long-running processes, at which the co-ordinator was able to allocate the processor to a more urgent process. Thus the system was not strictly run-to-completion.

Case (2) is the pre-emptive scheduling used in the multi-programming executive.

Case (3) is the simple round-robin in which all processes have the same priority.

The choice of scheduling strategy for the kernel is not clear-cut. Since we wish to simulate an environment in which arbitrary numbers of processes can run concurrently, we are drawn towards the round-robin. Against that, some processes are more important than others, and so we see a need for priority scheduling. But in any priority scheduling system there is a danger that a process may languish in the queue, never actually being run, and for this reason, priority-based systems may apply an 'ageing' factor to the priorities of processes currently in the purview of the scheduler, so that any process will sooner or later acquire sufficient priority to be run. While superficially reasonable, this technique has many dangers; in particular it may result in a 'user' process being run in preference to a vital system process. One *ad hoc* solution to this problem is to mark system processes as 'non-pre-emptable', so that they run to completion. Further disadvantages of pre-emptive priority scheduling are that response times may vary unpredictably, and it is difficult to handle numbers of 'user' processes which have intrinsically identical priorities. A satisfactory compromise can be achieved by using dynamic priorities: an elegant illustration of the technique is found in the UNIX system, which uses a pre-emptive priority algorithm modified as follows:

(1) All system processes have priorities that are greater than the highest user-process priority.
(2) User-process priorities are determined by the ratio of elapsed time to CPU time used over a fixed period, and are updated once per second, the scheduler being entered at the completion of the update.

Thus system processes always get preference over user processes, and a set of processor-bound user processes will run in a round-robin with a quantum of one second. The system is self-regulating: a process that is I/O bound will retain high priority, so ensuring a good response to interactive terminals, but when it changes from being I/O bound to

CPU-bound, its priority will fall rapidly. However, it will not be ignored entirely: while it is not using any processor time its priority will rise until eventually it will run again.

The extension of the scheduler to handle more than one processor is trivial: whenever the scheduler is entered it reallocates the available processors to the corresponding number of processes of highest priority in the queue. At first sight there seems to be a possible problem in ensuring that a processor is always available when required to run the scheduler or perform other system activity. In fact, the only problem arises with interrupts, since if a process halts voluntarily, the processor on which it was running necessarily becomes available for other purposes. As we have seen, interrupts are initially processed by the interrupt handler, which may then schedule a process to complete the servicing of the interrupt. The interrupt handler runs on whichever processor the interrupt is directed to by the hardware: if a process has to be scheduled, then the interrupted process will be placed on the waiting chain as if its time quantum had run out, and the processor so freed is used to run the scheduler. (We have assumed that the scheduler can be run on any available processor. Some multi-processor systems reserve one processor for system activity, but this is not a good idea, as it introduces an artificial asymmetry into the system.)

In the 'in-process' architecture, in which the scheduler, the interrupt handler and the rest of the kernel appear as part of every process image (virtual machine), any voluntary invocation of kernel activity (e.g. scheduling) will run as a procedure in the virtual machine that requested the activity: there is no pre-emption and no context switch. In a single-processor system interrupts are handled in the classical way, being dealt with in the virtual machine currently running. (Some systems, however, provide a separate stack for the interrupt handler so as to avoid the possiblity of stack overflow while dealing with an interrupt.) In a multi-processor system the hardware will direct particular interrupts to particular processors: otherwise much the same applies. In either case the interrupt handler identifies the interrupt, and if it is not relevant to the virtual machine in which the interrupt is being handled a message is sent to the appropriate virtual machine.

4.3 PROCESS COMMUNICATION AND SYNCHRONIZATION

We now have the ability to construct a system out of a number of autonomous processes. These run in a loosely-coupled manner: for much of the time they run independently, but from time to time they need to communicate. This communication can take several forms:

(1) *Signal* that some action has been performed.
(2) *Enquire* as to the status of some activity or process.
(3) Request to *wait* until some action has been performed.
(4) *Read* or *update* a shared data area.

(1) to (3) are generalizations of the communication between an interrupt routine and the interrupted program. (4) appears to be different. However, since access to shared data must at times be mutually exclusive (it is inadvisable to read data while another process is updating it) some communication is required to achieve this mutual exclusion.

4.3.1   The semaphore

Many different techniques are used to achieve process synchronization and mutual exclusion. A conceptually simple and easily implemented mechanism is the *semaphore* (invented by Dijkstra, and therefore sometimes called a 'Dijkstra semaphore'). A semaphore is a special kind of variable with the following properties:

(1) It can take only non-negative integral values.
(2) It can be operated on by only four operations, all of which are indivisible, i.e. once started they will be completed without interruption. The operations are:

   (i) *Set*: assign an initial value.
   (ii) *Test*: examine the value.
   (iii) *Wait*: decrease the value by one if this will yield a non-negative result. Otherwise wait until this can be done.
   (iv) *Signal*: increase the value by one.

(The Dutch words for 'wait' and 'signal' have inital leters P and V respectively. Hence Dijkstra calls the operations 'P' and 'V'.) The wait operation represents a potential delay: if the operation cannot be carried out the process trying to perform it will be halted, to restart (or more precisely to become free) when some other process performs a signal operation on the same semaphore. Thus a practical definition of wait(s) is:

```
if s > 0
then s := s − 1
else mark process halted
   and enter scheduler
{these operations being
performed without interruption}
```

We can now see how semaphores can be used for process communication.

(a) Waiting for something to be done

P1	P2
set(sem, 0)	.
start(P2)	.
wait(sem)	.
	.
	signal(sem)

P1 will halt on the wait, and will be freed by the signal at the end of P2.

Alternatively, P1 could test the semaphore to find out if P2 had finished:

P1	P2
set(sem, 0)	.
start(sem, 0)	.
	.
	signal(sem)
.	
.	
.	
if sem > 0	
then {P2 finished}	
else {P2 not finished}	

(b) The rendezvous

Processes P1 and P2 have to interact in some particular circumstance. Whichever reaches the critical point first must wait for the other.

{sem1 and sem2 set to zero}

P1	P2
.	.
.	.
.	.
signal(sem1)	signal(sem2)
wait(sem2)	wait(sem1)
*	*

(Note the vital importance of getting the *wait* and *signal* operations in the right order. What happens if the sequence is reversed?)

(c) Mutual exclusion

Processes P1, P2 require exclusive access to a shared resource, i.e. while

P1 is accessing the resource, P2 must be locked out, and vice versa.

P1   P2

{sem is initialized to 1}

wait(sem)

{access to   wait(sem)
resource}
                                  {access to
signal(sem)   resource}

                                  signal(sem)

Whichever process performs the wait operation first will be allowed to proceed. If the other process tries to access the shared resource before the first has issued the signal operation, it will be held at the wait operation.

(d) Claiming a resource

A process has to claim a resource before it can continue: processes are in competition for the resource, so the claiming must be done in an orderly manner. If the resource is not available the process must halt.

{sem1 initialized to 1 elsewhere}

set(sem2, 0)
wait(sem1)

claim resource: if
     successful signal(sem2)
signal(sem1)
wait(sem2)

Two semaphores are involved. sem1 provides mutual exclusion to ensure that two processes cannot try to claim the resource at the same time. If the resource is not available, the process will be halted by the wait(sem2): we assume that there is elsewhere a mechanism to signal(sem2) when the resource becomes available.

(e) The producer–consumer system

Process P1 generates information which is used by P2. The information

comes in fixed size units (e.g. lines, blocks) and there is a buffer large
enough to hold just one unit. P1 must halt when it has filled the buffer and
wait for P2 to empty it: P2 must wait for the buffer to be refilled after it has
processed the buffer contents.

P1	P2
repeat	repeat
fill buffer	wait(sem2)
signal(sem2)	process contents
	of buffer
wait(sem1)	signal(sem1)
indefinitely	indefinitely

It is tempting to believe that the producer–consumer situation requires
only one semaphore, but this is not so. sem2 acts as a 'buffer now full'
indicator, while sem1 indicates 'buffer now empty'. Both must be initialized to zero before P1 and P2 start. The example can be generalized to
deal with multiple buffers. Suppose that there are n buffers, initially all
empty. P1 need not halt until all n have been filled, and P2 must halt only
if no buffers are full. This can be ensured if sem1 is initialized to $n-1$ and
sem2 is initialized to zero.

It is sometimes convenient to distinguish between *global* and *private*
semaphores. Either kind can be associated with a group of processes.
The difference is that if a semaphore is global, all the processes in the
group are allowed to perform wait and signal operations on it, whereas
if it is private only one process may perform wait operations, though all
the processes in the group can perform signal operations. It will be clear
from the examples above that global semaphores are used for mutual
exclusion, and private semaphores are used for synchronization.

4.3.2 Implementation of semaphores

In the abstract, a semaphore is just a special variable with the properties
described above. In practice, we need to know when a process is waiting
on a semaphore, so that it can be freed when another process signals that
semaphore. A simple solution is to add another field to the process
descriptor to hold the *halt chain*, and to chain together all the processes
that are waiting on a particular semaphore. The semaphore itself
becomes a two-component item, containing the integer value and the
head of the halt chain. The data structures involved are illustrated in Fig.
4.1.

In many situations it suffices for a semaphore to take only two values,
zero and one. Such a semaphore is very easily implemented using a 'test
and set' instruction, and recent hardware designs (e.g. the Motorola

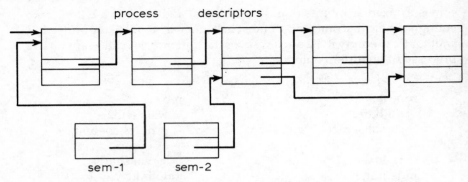

Fig. 4.1   Data structures for practical implementation of semaphores.

M68000) include such an instruction for just this purpose.

An essential limitation of semaphores as so far described is that a process can halt for only one reason at a time – it cannot ask that it be halted until one of a number of events occurs. This is a tolerable restriction, except in one particular case, *time-out*. We sometimes wish to say 'halt me until *either* event x occurs *or* a time t has elapsed, whichever happens first'. (For example, when driving a communication line, time-out can be used to detect a loss of connection somewhere in the telephone system.) A possible solution to the problem is to chain together the descriptors of processes that have a time-out requirement (using yet another field in the process descriptor), and to include in the descriptor a count called the *local clock*. This is initially set to the appropriate value: on each clock interrupt the local clocks of all processes on the time-out chain are decremented, and if any one reaches zero, that process is marked as free. Used in conjunction with a semaphore this gives the desired time-out facility; used on its own the local clock gives a 'sleep' facility, so that a process can be initiated after a fixed time. This is very useful for supervisory processes that need to run at fixed intervals.

4.4   PROTECTION

A process requires resources (processor, memory, devices, etc.), and resource allocation is an important part of operating system structure. The obverse of this coin is *protection*: a process must be able to access only those resources that have been allocated to it, and must not be able to access resources allocated to another process (unless they are explicitly shareable). Malfunction of a process must be contained within a firewall, and must not affect other processes.

In order to enforce protection it is essential to have hardware assistance. The simplest level of hardware assistance is to make some machine operations available only to programs running in a privileged 'system' mode, and to restrict access to certain processor registers and memory areas to programs in system mode. (Detailed methods of memory protection are discussed later.) A simple two-state system is rather crude, and one improvement is to generalize the system so as to have multiple 'levels' or 'rings' of protection. This approach was pioneered in the MULTICS system, and later adopted for ICL's larger 2900 series machines. Here there are sixteen protection levels, which can be envisaged as an onion-skin structure, with the highest privilege residing at the centre. A process operating in a particular ring can access memory segments belonging to processes in outer rings, but is prevented from accessing 'inwards' towards the centre. Thus user programs, running in an outer ring, cannot corrupt operating system procedures running in inner rings, but the kernel can manipulate data belonging to processes in the outer rings (as it must).

If the system is built round an 'in-process' architecture, protection is applied at the level of the procedure. Thus when a job requires an operating system function it calls a procedure that operates at a greater protection level. This inward call must be trapped, since it apparently violates the protection mechanism. It is necessary for the called procedure to vet the call, establishing that everything is in order before allowing the operation to proceed. When control returns to the calling procedure the protection level is restored to that which was set at the time of the procedure call, so that the user job carries on at its own protection level. The vetting of inward calls requires the maintenance of some sort of 'authority list', specifying who may do what, and to whom. The maintenance of such lists and the vetting of inward calls may impose a substantial overhead. VME/B attempts to minimize the overhead by maintaining system call tables which specify, for any protected procedure, the highest access level from which it can be called. (The procedure can of course make further checks itself, e.g. to verify the user identity.) This is a reasonably effective compromise, but it leaves a loophole in the protection, since if one procedure at a given level may reasonably make an inward call on a particular procedure, *all* procedures at that level can make a similar inward call.

It would evidently be convenient to have stronger protection with less overhead. Recent research has been directed to this end, and has developed a strategy of protection known as a 'capability architecture'. A *capability* is an unforgetable 'ticket', the mere possession of which constitutes undeniable authority for the holder to carry out operations (e.g. memory access) involving resources specified on the ticket, and in ways similarly specified on the ticket. Capabilities can be passed as procedure parameters, and in particular a calling procedure can pass a subset (but never a super-set) of its capabilities to the called procedure. Thus resource allocation can be achieved with complete protection in a hierarchical manner. This technique offers a substantial degree of protection, but its effective exploitation requires that the concept be built into the system at the hardware level and into the programming languages used for developing system software. It is still in the process of development, and for the most part confined to experimental machines at present.

5
Memory management

5.1 REQUIREMENTS FOR MEMORY MANAGEMENT

In our discussion of the kernel so far, we have tacitly assumed an infinite memory, taking it for granted that all the process images known to the system can be held in memory, available for execution when selected by the scheduler. This is unlikely to be the case in practice: at best only a subset of the process images can be held in memory at any one time, and on a small machine there may be room in main memory only for the currently executing process image. It is therefore necessary to have another layer of software in the operating system which stores process images on disc, and arranges for the appropriate images to be present in main memory when they are required. This is done in such a way that the process is not aware of the movement between disc and main memory – the memory management software presents an interface that simulates an apparently infinite memory.

Before going any further, we summarize the requirements of a memory management system. There are four major requirements, as follows.

(1) Protection: even if only one process-image is in memory at a time, it will be sharing the memory with the kernel, and it is imperative that a malfunction of the process should not overwrite kernel code or data. If more then one process image is in memory at any one time there is an additional need to enforce mutual protection between them.

(2) Transparency: memory allocation should be invisible to the process. If a process is halted for a long time we may wish to roll it out to the disc. (Indeed, some systems automatically roll out a process when-ever it halts.) The memory allocation should be such that the process can be rolled in to a *different* memory area without any special action within the process.

(3) Multiple segments: the process-image is logically composed of a number of *segments*: code, data, stack and system data. It may be required to have these segments in physically disjoint memory areas, though the code, stack and data segments must appear to be logically contiguous.

(4) Code sharing: if the code of a program is *invariant*, i.e. is not altered by the program, and if such a program is simultaneously part of two or more process images it may be desirable to keep a single physical copy of the code segment, which appears logically in all the appropriate process-images. (Such a program is commonly described as *re-entrant*: shareable code is sometimes described as *pure* code.)

It is possible (just) to implement an operating system on a machine with no hardware facilities for memory management. However, almost all operating systems make use of some hardware assistance in this area. The designer of the operating system is at the mercy of the hardware design in this respect: he has to make the best of what is provided. We shall therefore look at some typical hardware organizations, and see how they work, and the sort of memory management that can be provided.

5.2 PROTECTION KEYS

One of the earliest forms of hardware assistance for memory management was found in the IBM System/360 (later System/370). A 4-bit *storage protection lock* is associated with each block of 2048 bytes of memory. Each executing program has a 4-bit *protection key* as part of the processor status word (PSW), which can only be set by a privileged instruction (i.e. by the kernel, since all other programs run in normal mode). Memory accesses are vetted by the hardware, and are only permitted if the program key matches the lock of the block in question. (Key zero acts as a skeleton key, allowing privileged code unrestricted access to the whole of the memory.) Memory is partitioned by assigning a particular lock code to a number of contiguous blocks. It is thus easy to divide memory into a fixed number of partitions of fixed size, and the technique is thus well adapted to the implementation of a fixed-partition multi-stream spooling system. However, this technique does not meet the other requirements. The major disadvantage is that the program must be loaded into a partition at the appropriate absolute address by the relocating loader, and once loaded it cannot easily be moved elsewhere in memory. This makes it difficult, though not impossible, to implement a dynamic system with a varying number of processes.

5.3 MEMORY MAPPING

Practical memory management systems for modern operating systems are based on the idea of *memory mapping*. In this we distinguish between the *logical address space* seen by an executing program and the *physical address space* of the actual memory. On every memory reference the hardware maps the logical address supplied by the program into a corresponding physical address. This mapping can be done in a number of ways in order to meet the requirements set out above. It is desirable that the address mapping should always be effective when the processor is running in normal mode, but capable of being disabled by programs running in system mode. The registers defining the mapping should likewise be accessible only in system mode, so that once set up the mapping cannot be affected by a 'user' process.

5.3.1 Bank switching

This is a crude type of memory mapping found on some microprocessor systems. Typically, a *bank selection register* can be set to specify one of eight physical memory banks. Bank 0 contains 64k bytes, while banks 1 to 7 each contain 48k bytes. When a program generates a memory access in the range 0 to 48k the hardware directs it to the bank specified by the bank selection register. Addresses above 48k are always directed to bank zero. Thus an operating system can reside in the top 16k of memory with up to eight different program stores in the physical memory with complete mutual protection. When the system wishes to run another program it merely resets the bank selection register accordingly. This type of memory management is used in the MP/M multi-user version of CP/M.

5.3.2 Base-limit addressing

Bank switching is a crude memory management technique, and is restricted to a fixed number of 'user' programs. For operating systems it is desirable to be able to cope with the allocation of variable numbers of memory segments of varying sizes. A simple and effective form of memory mapping to meet this requirement is *base-limit addressing*. This technique is used by a number of mainframes including ICL 1900, UNIVAC 1100, Honeywell 6000 and the earlier models of the DEC10. The processor (each processor in a multi-processor system) is equipped with a pair of registers that define a mapping. Let these be denoted by B and L. Mapping of logical addresses is carried out as follows.

Let N be the address presented to the memory (after indexing and/or indirection, and let b, l be the contents of B and L respectively. If $N > l$ the memory access is illegal, and suitable action is taken. Otherwise the address N is mapped into $N + b$.

Thus the logical address space $0 . . . l$ is mapped on to the physical addresses $b . . . b + l$. The mapping provides protection, since any attempt by the process to address outside its bounds $(0 . . . l)$ will be trapped. The mapping is transparent: the physical memory used can be changed but provided the contents of B are also changed the process will be unaware of the move. In its simplest form, however, base-limit addressing does not provide multiple segments or code-sharing.

At start-up, the kernel will occupy part of the physical memory, and the rest of the memory will be free. As processes are created they are placed in the next available memory position. The process descriptor holds the address at which the process-image starts, and its length, so that when the process is scheduled for execution, the B and L registers can be loaded to map addresses on to the right part of memory. Each time a process dies a 'gap' will be created in the memory. Thus the memory will develop a 'chequerboard' effect, occupied regions alternating with unused gaps. The memory management routines must therefore administer this pool of free memory gaps, and respond to requests in a reasonably efficient manner. To do this we maintain a 'free list' which records the start address and length of each free gap in memory. When a new process is created, a suitable gap must be choosen for its process-image to occupy. The address of the chosen gap is recorded in the process descriptor, along with the length of the process image, and the free store list is updated to reflect the fact that the gap is smaller (or non-existent, if the new process image just fits). When a process dies, the base and limit fields in the descriptor define the gap created; this is coalesced with adjacent gaps if necessary, and the free storage list updated. The only problem left is how to choose a 'suitable' gap to meet a request

What is a suitable gap? To optimize occupancy we ought to find a gap that exactly fits the process image, or failing that, the smallest gap that exceeds the required size. (The remaining unoccupied space is then recorded in the free-store list as a small gap.) This is called the *best-fit* algorithm. To implement this method it is desirable that the free-store list should be sorted by size of gap so that the appropriate gap can be located quickly. Thus each time a new gap is created the list has to be reordered, and the resultant overheads are non-trivial, especially if processes are created, or their images moved, at all frequently. Many systems therefore adopt the *first-fit* algorithm, i.e. they use the first gap that is large enough. The danger of this approach is that we finish up with a lot of moderate-size gaps, none of which is big enough for a process image. Using the best-fit algorithm reduces the size of the wasted gaps, but in either case we generate unusable areas of memory. This is the phenomenon of *memory fragmentation*. Eventually the point will be reached at which there is no gap large enough for a new process to be installed, although the sum of the gaps may exceed the space required. There are now two possibilities: either the loading of the process has to wait until a suitable gap appears, or we may *compact* the memory, moving all the process images into a contiguous area, so that the gaps coalesce into one big gap at the end. This is possible because the base-limit mapping is entirely transparent, but the overhead can be horrendous if compacting takes place at all frequently. The problem of fragmentation is alleviated if the requirement for large contiguous blocks is reduced. There is thus some advantage in allocating code and data areas separately, and some machines (e.g. UNIVAC 1100) facilitate this by providing two base-limit register pairs, one for instruction accesses and one for data accesses.

In practice, the total memory requirements of all the processes known to the system will greatly exceed the actual memory available. It is therefore necessary to adopt a more positive approach to memory management, moving process images out of memory on to disc to create space for a new process, and later bringing the process images back. This procedure is known as *roll-out* and *roll-in*. Space may be required either to install a new process, or to reinstate a process that has been rolled out. If no suitable gap can be found, a process must be selected for roll-out. The obvious candidates are those processes that are halted. We therefore examine all such processes, compute the space that would be made available by roll-out (taking account of existing gaps on either side) and choose a suitable process. Here again we can use either best-fit or first-fit as our criterion for selection. Elaborate algorithms have been devised for administering memory under this kind of regime, but large mainframes nowadays use a more sophisticated technique of memory mapping known as paging (discussed later), and so we do not discuss the algorithms further. Base-limit mapping is usually found in minicomputers, and since the memory will typically be large enough for only a few process images to be resident a more extreme allocation strategy is usually employed. Immediately the currently-running process halts it is rolled out. This ensures that there is (almost) always space to roll in a process, or to start a new process.

5.3.3 Memory mapping in the PDP11

The memory mapping of the PDP11 is typical of the technique used in 16-bit minicomputers. Memory mapping was originally introduced in these machines as a way of escaping from the constraints of a 16-bit address space, but we will describe it from the point of view of operating system development. (In fact, the following description applies strictly only to the mid-range PDP11s. The larger models in the range have more elaborate memory mapping, but the principle remains the same.)

The basic function of the memory management is to map the 64k address space seen by the program on to one or more segments of a larger physical memory. The address space is notionally divided into eight *pages* each of 8k bytes. An address can thus be thought of as being divided into a page number and a displacement in page, thus:

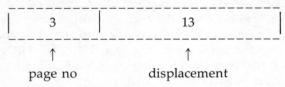

The hardware includes two *page tables*, one to be used in normal mode and one to be used in system mode. Each page table contains eight *page address registers* (PARs). The physical memory is likewise notionally divided into 8k pages, and each PAR holds (*inter alia*) the number of a physical page. Since the maximum memory size is 256k, there are at most 32 pages, so the page number held in the PAR is a 5-bit quantity. The memory mapping uses the top three bits of the address (the page number) to select one of the eight PARs, then replaces those three bits by the five bits from the PAR, generating an 18-bit actual address. By setting the PARs suitably, each page of the logical address space can be mapped on to a page of physical memory. A simple use is to map contiguous areas of logical address space on to contiguous areas of physical memory: by changing the PARs during the context switch we can keep several process images, and the kernel, in physical memory simultaneously with full protection and transparency. Another common use of the PARs relates to control of the addresses normally used to address the peripheral devices. In, the PDP11 architecture the control registers for the peripherals, appear in the highest page of the physical memory, and if a process has access to them the PARs must map the last 8k bytes of the process address space on to this physical page. If the eighth PAR is not set, there is no way in which the program can access the device control registers. Usually, the eighth PAR is set in the system mode tables to map on to the device control addresses in physical memory, but is not so set in the user mode tables. This restricts peripheral access to programs running in system mode. It is possible to set the user mode eighth PAR to map on to a page of physical memory, thus making it possible to use the whole of the 64k address space.

As a further refinement the PARs include a second field, the *limit*, which specifies how much of the page is actually usable, and a protection field that allows a page to be marked as read-only. Using the limit field a memory of any size can be mapped at the expense of wasting part of the last page. On average we will lose 4k per process image: this is not too serious because the limited memory restricts the number of process images that can be stored, anyway. (Note that this waste is not the same as the fragmentation we have discussed previously. The unused part of the last page is completely inaccessible: we have defined a mapping with holes.) Used in this way, the PDP11 memory mapping is equivalent to base-limit addressing. The larger PDP11s have separate sets of PARs for instruction and data access ('separate I–D space'): on these systems it is possible to allocate data and code areas separately.

The hardware mechanisms of the PDP11 allow us to carry out more sophisticated mapping than simple base-limit, since the contiguous address space seen by the programmer can be mapped on to disjoint areas of physical memory. This ability is exploited in UNIX, whose memory management we now discuss.

5.4   UNIX MEMORY MANAGEMENT

A UNIX process image consists of two logically separate parts, a read-only code segment, and a data segment (including the stack). These must appear to occupy contiguous memory while the process is executing, but there is advantage in using the PDP11's PARs to map two disjoint areas of physical memory, since the memory allocation routines will find it easier to accommodate two smaller segments than a single large segment. A process image also includes a small amount of *system data*. The PDP11 uses a separate stack for operations in system mode: the system data segment holds this stack, together with space to dump the processor registers, PSW and open file descriptors when the process is not actually running. This segment must be accessible to the operating system but must be protected from the process when running in normal ('user') mode; such protection is readily achieved by mapping it only in the system mode PARs. By convention, the system data is mapped in the seventh PAR in system mode, and so appears at addresses 48k to 56k. Only this PAR needs to be changed in the system registers as part of a context switch. The user-mode PARs are set so that the code appears at the low end of the memory, with the data segment immediately above it (on a page boundary). The stack starts at the highest physical address (FFFF) and extends downwards through the eighth page (and the seventh if need be). The stack and data areas are extended dynamically to meet requirements.

5.4.1   Swapping

Since the PDP11 memory is small compared with the memory requirements of all processes known to the system, process images are regarded as normally resident on disc, and are brought into main memory as required on a first-fit basis. (The process descriptor block is expanded to include a resident/non-resident flag and a disc address to record the location of an out-of-memory process image.) The moving of process images between disc and main memory is the responsibility of a continuously running *swapping process*. This scans the process-descriptor chain looking for a process that is marked 'free' but is not currently in main memory. If there are two or more such processes the one that has been swapped out for the longest time is selected. The swapping process now attempts to find suitable gaps in memory to accommodate the process image to be swapped in: if there is insufficient space it selects a resident process image to swap out. All halted processes are candidates for removal, with preference being given to processes waiting on 'slow' events (i.e. not disc I/O). If there is more than one candidate, a first-in first-out rule is applied. This swapping out is repeated if necessary until enough free space has been created to swap in the selected process image. This relatively simple algorithm gives quite good performance: if main memory is very limited it automatically becomes a total swapping algorithm, with process images being swapped out as soon as the process halts.

5.5   PAGED MEMORY

Many medium to large computers use a mapping technique called *paging* for memory management. (This should not be confused with the techniques used on the PDP11, despite the use of the word 'page' in both contexts. Terminology in this area is particularly confusing.) The initial motivation of paging is to solve the problem of fragmentation that occurs in base-limit addressing, by mapping contiguous logical space on to *small* disjoint areas of physical memory. The basic idea is to divide the memory into *page frames* of fixed size, typically sizes lying between 512 and 2048 bytes. The logical address space seen by the user is divided into *pages* of the same size as the page frames, and an address generated by a program is interpreted as a page number and a displacement within the page. A *page table* maps page numbers on to page frames, thus achieving the desired mapping on to disjoint memory areas. The mapping process is illustrated in Fig. 5.1.

As it stands, the technique is not viable because of the size of the page table – 1024 entries for a 1/2 megabyte machine with a 512 byte page frame. A page table of such a size is too expensive to implement in hardware, and in any case the overhead of reloading it on every context switch is too large to accept. It is neccessary to keep the page table in memory as part of the process image, and a processor register points to the page table for the currently executing process. Only this register needs to be changed as part of the context switch. However, we have replaced the overhead in the context switch by an overhead on every

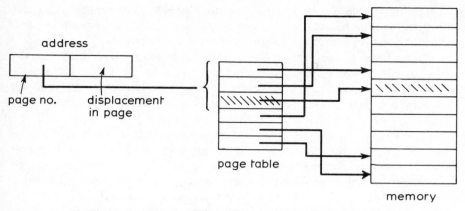

address

page no.   displacement
              in page

page table

memory

Fig. 5.1 Mapping of memory in a paged system.

virtual memory reference, since we now need two physical memory references, one to get the page mapping and a second to get the actual information required. Fortunately, we can alleviate this by another hardware device that takes account of the fact that memory references exhibit a degree of *locality*: programs do not address the memory in a random fashion, and there is a reasonable probability that if a page has been accessed, it will be accessed again in the near future. We therefore provide a *translation buffer* consisting of a set of registers, each of which can hold a page number and the physical address of the corresponding page. These registers hold the n most recent mappings (values of n of 64 or 128 are typical). These registers can be examined very rapidly, and on each memory reference the paging hardware checks to see if the page number is already recorded in the translation buffer. If it is, the mapping is retrieved immediately; if not, the page table is consulted and the mapping is recorded in the translation buffer, overwriting an earlier entry. The registers of the translation buffer are loaded in a cyclic fashion so that they always record the most recent page accesses. In practice this technique is remarkably effective, and 'hit rates' of 90% can be achieved. However, since the translation buffer must be cleared at every context switch the effective hit rate is somewhat lower. The translation buffer is an example of an associative memory, since it is addressed by specifying the content of the desired register, not an address. Such a memory is expensive to implement in hardware, and many systems use a simpler technique in which the mapping is stored in the translation buffer at a position determined by taking the virtual address modulo the translation buffer size. (Since this simply means that the buffer address is determined by taking bits from the least significant end of the address it is very easy to implement in hardware.) Using this technique it cannot be guaranteed that the buffer will contain the last n references, since the registers of the buffer are not filled sequentially. To compensate for this, the translation buffer is usually made of larger capacity.

In addition to performing the mapping, the page table entries usually include access controls. Typically, three bits are provided to indicate whether the page can be written to, and whether it can be read for instruction fetch, data fetch or both. (This makes it possible to have 'execute-only' pages as well as 'read-only' pages.)

The paging system as described solves the problem of memory fragmentation that was apparent in the simple base-limit system, but its cost would scarcely by justified if that were all it did. In practice, paged memory is rather different. As described, the paging system maps a virtual address space on to a physical address space *of the same size*. (By contrast, PDP11 memory mapping maps a program's virtual address space on to a *much larger* physical address space.) Paging is usually organized to provide a logical address space which is *much larger* than the physical memory, giving each process a very large *virtual memory*. Obviously, the virtual memory contents cannot all be in real memory; it is necessary to store some of the pages on disc, and to arrange somehow that pages are brought into physical memory as required. Why do this? Manufacturer's literature suggests that in this way the end user can be given access to a much larger memory than is actually provided by the main memory. While this is a useful facility for certain very large scientific computations, it would be foolhardy to try to run a system on the basis of offering users more memory than was actually available – you never get something for nothing. The real benefit of a large virtual memory is that it allows programmers and system designers to place data structures of uncertain size at well-separated addresses, so removing the danger of overlap. For example, a common technique used in the implementation of Pascal is to place the code at the 'bottom' of the memory, and to have a heap growing upwards from the top of the code and a stack growing downwards from the top of the memory. If the total memory slot is too small there is a danger that the heap and stack will collide, but if we allocate a large slot there is a danger that memory space will be unused, and therefore wasted. A virtual memory allows us to allocate a large slot so that the stack and the heap are well separated, removing the danger of collision. At the same time, nothing is wasted, since if the pages between the heap and the stack are not referenced they will not be brought into main memory, and the overhead of their existence is trivial.

To implement this kind of virtual memory the page tables are extended to include an extra bit signalling 'resident' or 'non-resident'. For a resident page the page table gives the memory address as before: for a non-resident page the page table contains the *disc* address. We postpone for a short time a discussion of what happens when a program tries to access a non-resident page, and attend to more pressing problems.

If each process has access to a large virtual memory, its page table is potentially very large also, and subject to variation in size if the process changes its memory requirement. How can we store the page tables, and allow for variation in size, without tying up an excessive amount of memory? The answer is to store the page tables themselves in virtual memory. This sounds like magic, but we shall now see how it can be accomplished in safety.

5.5.1   Paging on the VAX11

By way of illustration we describe the organization of the memory management hardware of the DEC VAX11 machines (omitting a certain amount of detail irrelevant to our present purpose). The VAX has a 32-bit address, and the virtual address space seen by a program is thus $2**32$ bytes. Of this space, the upper half is common to all processes: this is called *system space*. The lower half of the virtual address space is separately defined for each process: this is called *process space*. Process space is further subdivided into two regions of equal size, P0 which grows upwards from address zero, and P1 which grows downwards from the highest address ($2**31 - 1$). This facilitates the use of the standard technique of letting code grow from the bottom of memory while the stack grows down from the top of the memory. The virtual memory is divided into 512-byte pages, the physical memory being correspondingly divided into 512-byte pages, and separate page tables are provided for system space, P0 process space and P1 process space. Since the actual size of the system space (as opposed to the theoretical upper limit of $2**31$ bytes) is relatively constant, and known at system-generation time, the system page table is allocated a fixed amount of space in physical memory. Processor registers define the base and size of the system page table. Page tables for process space are allocated on a per-process basis in virtual memory, in system space; two pairs of registers define the base and limit for the P0 and P1 space of the current process (as virtual addresses). Only these registers need be reloaded on a context switch. In the worst case address mapping for process space addresses is a lengthy operation – we have to access the system page table to map the contents of the page-table base and limit registers, then use the process page table so located to find the actual page address. Clearly, the system will only be viable if an effective translation buffer is provided. The VAX hardware in fact provides separate translation buffers for system space and process space: this gives a substantial benefit since the system space buffer does not need to be cleared on a context switch.

5.5.2 Memory management with paging

In a paged system each process image occupies a number of pages in the virtual memory space. The total amount of virtual memory occupied by all the processes known to the system will greatly exceed the physical memory available, though each process will require only a fraction of its virtual memory to be available at any instant. We therefore think of process images as being normally resident on disc, and the function of the memory management is to bring pages of active process images into main memory as required. Luckily, a process will normally require only a small part of the total process image in main memory at any one time. This is a consequence of the property of locality already discussed. The more page frames that are allocated to a process, the more likely we are to find the required page for a given memory access in main memory. However, if we were to plot the frequency of requests for a page not already in physical memory against the number of page frames allocated to that process we would find that there is a critical point beyond which an increase in the number of page frames allocated makes very little difference to the frequency of requests for pages to be brought into main memory. This critical point occurs when the set of pages currently being accessed is all located in real memory. This set of pages is called the *working set*. Clearly, the objective of memory management must be to retain the working sets of all active processes in main memory. Three substantial problems stand in the way of achieving this:

(1) It is impossible to determine the working set of a process *a priori*.
(2) In any case, the working set changes with time.
(3) The sum of the working sets of all active processes may exceed the physical memory space available.

Before detailing the mechanisms used by the memory management routines, we look at some general considerations regarding paged memory. When a process tries to access a page that is not in physical memory a *page fault* interrupt is generated. The interrupt handler activates the memory management routines, which halt the requesting process on a semaphore and enter a request for the page to be retrieved from disc. The semaphore is passed as a parameter so that the halted process can be freed when the page is available. If there are unused page frames in memory the operation is straightforward, but typically all the physical memory is occupied, so that it is necessary to select a page to be evicted: this selection is the province of the *page-turning algorithm* or *replacement algorithm*. This algorithm is the key to efficient operation of a paged system. If the algorithm habitually removes pages that are currently active it will generate a lot of needless traffic to and from the disc, a phenomenon known as *thrashing*.

The job of the replacement algorithm is to select a page frame to be used to accommodate the in-coming page of virtual memory, overwriting the existing page of virtual memory. The first stage in designing such an algorithm is to identify the candidates for removal. There are two strategies: *global replacement* and *per-process replacement*. With global replacement *all* pages resident in real memory (except *locked down* system pages) are candidates for replacement. On the other hand the per-process replacement strategy guarantees that when a process needs another page frame *one of its own pages* will be chosen for replacement. If this strategy is used each active process is allocated a *quota* of real memory: page requests are met from this quota, and when the quota is exhausted page requests result in an existing page being overwritten. The disadvantage of per-process replacement is that the choice of an appropriate quota is difficult, and a fixed quota takes no account of the varying size of the working set. The result is that some processes finish up with more real memory then they need, while others cannot accommodate the working set within their quota, and thrashing results. A dynamically adjusted quota goes some way towards alleviating this problem. Global replacement is simpler to administer, but is open to criticism on the grounds that the progress of a particular process is not determined solely by its own pattern of memory accesses, but by a complex and unpredictable interaction between the memory access patterns of all the active processes in the system.

Whichever strategy is adopted, the next decision to be made is whether to try to anticipate paging requirements, or whether to let the paging be 'event driven', fetching pages as required with no attempt to forecast the pattern of requests. This technique is known as 'demand paging', and is very commonly used.

The decision on demand paging determines when pages may be transferred, and the local/global replacement decision determines the possible candidates for replacement. The final decision is *which* page should be chosen for replacement. We could make a random choice, but this is unlikely to be an optimum strategy. An easy-to-implement strategy is first-in first-out, but this is equivalent to removing the 'oldest' page, and if a program is in an intensive small loop within a page that page would be bound to be removed, although it was being used intensively. (We shall see later how it is possible to alleviate the worst results of first-in first-out replacement.) Ideally, the page to choose is that one which will not be used for the longest time, since its absence will make no difference in the short term. Since computers are not gifted with prescience this is impossible – the choice can only be based on past behaviour. An intuitively attractive strategy is to remove the least recently used page (LRU replacement), since the property of locality suggests that the probability of accessing a page is greater if it has been used in the recent past. Unfortunately, to implement LRU replacement it is necessary to keep a record of the use of each page frame, and this record must be updated on every memory access. Without special-purpose hardware (which no current commercially available machines provide) the overhead of maintaining this record makes LRU too costly to implement. Similar arguments rule out a strategy that chooses the least frequently used page frame for replacement (LFU replacement). Typically, the hardware will record in the page table entry the fact that a virtual page has been referenced, by setting a 'use bit', and whether the page has been written to by setting the 'modified bit' (sometimes called the 'dirty bit'). Given this level of hardware support, the best that can be done is to select for replacement a page that has not been used in the recent past: this is the 'not recently used' (NRU) strategy, and is a reasonable approximation to LRU in practice.

NRU replacement is relatively simple to implement if per-process replacement is the chosen strategy. When a page is first brought into physical memory the use bit and dirty bit in the page table entry are set to zero. When a page fault occurs, the page table for the currently executing process can be examined, and the pages can be divided into three categories:

(1) Unreferenced and unmodified.
(2) Referenced but unmodified.
(3) Referenced and modified.

Pages in category (1) are prime candidates for removal: if there are no pages in this category a page from category (2) should be chosen, since the contents of the page frame will not need to be written back to disc. As a last resort a page from category (3) will have to be chosen. If there are several possible pages to choose from in a particular category a random choice can be made, or a last-in first-out rule can be applied. This of course requires that a record has been kept of the order in which pages were loaded. As described, the NRU strategy is not very satisfactory, since as time progresses more and more of the pages will be referenced, so the number of pages in category (1) will fall to zero. It is necessary at intervals to force all the use bits to zero; this will give rise to an apparent anomaly in that there will be pages that appear to be unused but modified. Since the replacement algorithm will always try to avoid replacing a modified page, these anomalous pages can be considered to belong to category (3).

NRU replacement is more complicated if a global replacement strategy is in force. The page tables map virtual addresses on to physical page-frames. To administer NRU replacement we need a partial inverse mapping, since memory management deals with physical page frames and needs to know who is using them. This mapping takes the form of a table called the Memory Block Table (MBT). This has one entry per physical page, and is therefore indexed by page-frame number. Each entry contains the following fields:

Status: (free, in transit to/from disc, allocated)
Process-id: points to processor descriptor
Fixed flag: (pageable, locked down)
Reference bit: use described below

The NRU algorithm uses a 'removal pointer' which indexes a particular entry in the MBT. Initially it is set to point to the first entry, and all the reference bits in the MBT are set to zero. When a page fault interrupt occurs, actions are as follows:

(1) For each allocated block, consult the page table to see of the block has been referenced, and set the reference bit in the MBT accordingly.
(2) Advance the removal pointer to the next entry in the MBT (treating the table as circular, and skipping over locked-down pages).
(3) If the reference bit is zero then select this page for removal, otherwise set the reference bit to zero and repeat from (2).

It will be seen that this algorithm will select a not recently used page if one exists, also step (3) guarantees that the algorithm cannot loop. Having selected a page frame we check the page table to see if it has been written to: if so it is written back to disc. In any case the page table entry is amended to show that the page is non-resident, and if a reference to this page appears in the translation buffer it is removed. Finally the new page is brought in from the disc and the appropriate page table is updated before signalling via the semaphore to the process whose memory access started the whole procedure.

5.5.3 VAX/VMS memory management

Demand paging with NRU global replacement is conceptually very simple, but in practice can lead to poor performance if the physical memory is not large enough to hold the working sets of all active processes. Moreover, it is difficult to predict the behaviour of such a system, or to make rational decisions about resource allocation to improve performance. A very different strategy is used in VAX/VMS, and this is now described.

VAX/VMS uses two distinct mechanisms to control and optimize memory use. Paging is viewed primarily as a mechanism that allows a process image access to a large address space, so avoiding problems of collision when memory areas have to expand dynamically, and as a way of making system facilities available to all processes on a shared basis by placing procedures and tables at fixed addresses in system space. Sharing of physical memory amongst a large number of processes is achieved by having process images resident on disc, rolling them in when required and rolling them out when no longer active.

When the system is first booted, some pages are locked down (i.e. made permanently resident in physical memory) for system use: the remaining page frames are placed on a *free list*. When a process is created it is allocated a page quota, and its process-space page tables are set up with all pages marked non-resident (i.e. on disc). As page faults occur, pages are allocated from the free list (for the moment assumed to be inexhaustible) as long as the process has not used its quota. The addresses of the page frames allocated to a process are recorded in the *working set list*. This is organized as a circular list, so that when the process's quota is exhausted, the replacement algorithm can select a page on the first-in first-out basis. The VAX hardware does not provide a use bit in the page table entries, only a dirty bit, so there is little point in trying to implement any other selection rule. However, various steps are taken to avoid the potentially harmful consequences of first-in first-out replacement. If the page selected for removal has not been modified it is placed at the *end* of the free list; if it has been modified it is placed at the *end* of a 'modified page list'. Placing an unmodified page at the end of the free list ensures that it will not be immediately allocated to another process. The system delays writing the pages on the modified page list back to disc as long as possible. Thus, in either case, if a process refers to a recently removed page it is likely that the page will not have been reused, so it can be returned to the working set lists of the process with little trouble. This prevents the first-in first-out replacement removing a page that is referenced regularly over a long period.

The pages on the modified page list are not written to disc until the list reaches a specified threshold. At this point the pages are written, and the page frames returned to the end of the free list. In addition to the benefit already noted, this delayed write-back has further potential efficiency gains. If a page is referenced, and so recovered from the modified list, then modified again before being selected for removal, both modifications are accounted for in one write-back operation. In addition, accumulating a large number of page frames before writing back makes it possible to choose the sequence of writing to minimize head movement on the disc, and permits pages that are contiguous in virtual memory to be written to contiguous areas on disc, with possible benefits next time these pages have to be fetched from disc. As a final refinement, not all the pages on the modified page list are written to the disc at any one time. The last few pages are left until next time, thus maintaining the function of the list as a cache for recently used pages.

Meanwhile, what of the swapper? This is a separate process that runs at high priority (and is never itself swapped out, for obvious reasons). Its function is to ensure that the working sets of the highest priority processes that are currently free are available in physical memory. The swapper is activated (woken up) whenever a swapped-out process changes state and becomes free. The swapper must now find enough free pages for the working set list of this process. It first tries to satisfy the request from the free list (leaving a predetermined number of free pages still available to satisfy paging requests). In the likely event that there are insufficient pages on the free list, it next writes the modified page list pages back to disc (again leaving the 'cache' pages at the end of the list), thus topping up the free list. Finally, if the requests still cannot be satisfied it will swap out a process-image of equal or lower priority (preferring a process that is halted to one that is free).

This is a very simplified account of the VAX/VMS memory management system, but it will serve to illustrate the kinds of strategy that have to be adopted, and the decisions that have to be made, in the design of a real system.

5.6   SEGMENTATION

The final memory-allocation regime discussed is one known as 'segmentation'. Since the word 'segment' has been used in other contexts, it is better described as 'segmented virtual memory'.

The paged memory described above meets most of our objectives, with the exception of code-sharing. Sharing is a theoretical possibility, since two different page-table entries can point to the same physical page frame. However, the administration of a paged memory (in particular the replacement algorithm) requires a one-to-one correspondence between resident pages of virtual memory and physical page frames, thus making sharing a practical impossibility. A limited amount of code-sharing can be achieved in some cases. For example, in the VAX11 the upper half of the virtual memory (the system space) is common to all process images, so code in this area can be shared without violating the one-to-one correspondence rule. System procedures are sited at known, fixed addresses in virtual memory, and all processes calling them use the same virtual address.

The motivation of segmented virtual memory is to extend this sharing to *all* code. Segmentation provides a two-dimensional addressing system in virtual memory, thus a virtual address is made up of two parts, a segment number and the displacement within a segment. Unlike pages, which are of fixed size, segments can be of arbitrary length to suit the problem at hand. A segment table is maintained for each process, containing for each segment known to the process the (virtual) address of the start of the segment, and its size. A processor register points to the segment table for the currently executing process. The first stage in address translation is to use the segment table to verify the displacement, and then to generate the virtual address of the required data object. This mapping is illustrated in Fig. 5.2.

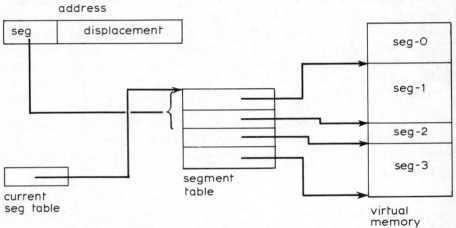

Fig. 5.2   Mapping of virtual address by segment table.

The result of this stage of translation is still a virtual address; in most segmented systems the segments are themselves paged to avoid fragmentation of physical memory. The address produced by the segment translation is divided into page number and displacement in a familiar way, and the final mapping is through a page table. (Note, however, that we now have a page table *per-segment* rather then per-process. The whole mapping is shown in Fig. 5.3.

The full translation process needs at least two extra memory references, so the overheads are appreciable. Fortunately, the use of a translation buffer reduces them to acceptable proportions. (The buffer works just like a paging translation buffer, but records the mapping from the original (segmented) virtual address to the final physical address.)

The original implementation of segmentation on the GE (later Honeywell) MULTICS system was exceedingly complex. The MULTICS philosophy was that segments could be called in an arbitrary manner:

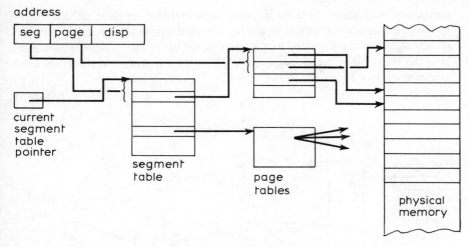

Fig. 5.3 Mapping of addresses in a segmented virtual memory.

indeed, files and segments were regarded as interchangeable. Since segments were identified by symbolic names, it was necessary to effect a run-time binding of segment names to segment numbers. This was difficult to achieve, and gave rise to the scurrilous rumour that the acronym MULTICS stood for 'Many Unnecessarily Large Tables in Core Store'. Therefore, later segmented systems used a compromise that facilitates code-sharing without producing all the complications of the MULTICS scheme.

The segmentation scheme of the ICL 2900 series is typical of the genre. Virtual addresses, as before, are made up of a segment number and displacement, and the mapping is done exactly as described. Unlike MULTICS, however, segments are not given symbolic names. It will be recalled that the VME system is based on an in-process architecture with a relatively small number of virtual machines (processes). When a virtual machine is created the kernel sets up its segment table, and system software writers have to establish a convention about segment numbers so that each program knows the segment numbers it should use. Code sharing is provided in two ways. In addition to normal (private) segments, segments can also be designated *public* or *global*. Public segments appear in all virtual machines, and are distinguished by having the most significant bit of the virtual address set to one (i.e. the top half of the virtual memory is the same for all VMs). A single segment table (the public segment table) performs the mapping for these segments. Global segments are shared by two or more VMs. The normal segment table entries contain a bit to mark a global segment: if this bit is set, the segment table entry is treated as an indirect address, pointing to an entry in the *shared segment table.* Thus a shared segment can appear at different virtual addresses for different users, yet its mapping to real memory is contained in a single entry in the shared segment table, thus making it easy to move it if need be. The VME segmentation mechanisms are summarized in Fig. 5.4.

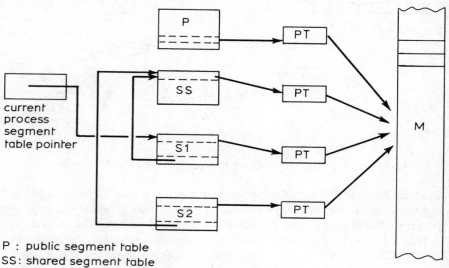

P : public segment table
SS: shared segment table
S1, S2 : segment tables for specific processes
M : memory

Fig. 5.4 Segmentation in VME.

6
Discs and files

6.1 SOME GENERAL CONSIDERATIONS

We must now turn our attention to the general area of input–output (I/O), traditionally one of the most messy aspects of programming and certainly one of the less tractable areas of operating system design. The reason is that input–output brings us inexorably up against the real world. In most of the operating system we can define our own interfaces to suit our requirements: with I/O we are stuck with whatever the hardware provides.

It is convenient to separate discussion of I/O into two parts, dealing first with discs and then with terminal devices and printers, etc. Discs are *block devices* which handle information transfers in fixed-size blocks, and in concurrent systems they are also *shared*, being accessed by a number of processes. In contrast, terminals and printers are *character* devices (the unit of transfer is a single byte) and are *non-shared*, 'belonging' to a single process at any one time. (It is possible, though not easy, in the UNIX system to get oneself by accident into a situation where two processes are sharing access to the keyboard. The resulting confusion has to be experienced to be believed.)

6.1.1 Logical, physical and device-level I/O

In a simple operating system discs are used only to store files (which may contain text or executable code). In a more complex system the discs are also used to hold pages of virtual memory, and/or swapped-out process images. These two uses of discs are somewhat different. The hardware designer will ensure that the page size in virtual memory bears a simple relationship to the block size on disc, and in a simple swapping system the software designer will take care that the swapping unit corresponds to an integral number of disc blocks. On the other hand, users' files and system files are of variable and varying size; they are essentially arbitrary length byte sequences, and the block structure of the disc has to be superimposed on these sequences. These two conflicting requirements are reconciled by providing an extra layer of software, and we distinguish two levels of I/O activity, *logical* I/O and *physical* I/O.

(1) *Physical* I/O is input–output in which the unit of transfer matches the physical unit appropriate to the device, e.g. tracks from a disc.
(2) *Logical* I/O is input–output in programmer's terms, where the programmer sees an abstract device that is more convenient to his purpose than a physical device, e.g. viewing the disc not as fixed-length tracks but as variable-length files.

Once again the software forms a hierarchy: the logical I/O routines map arbitrary length files on to sequences of fixed-size blocks, and call the physical I/O routines to transfer information a block at a time. In fact, it is convenient to provide a further layer of software between the physical I/O and the actual discs, the *device-level* I/O. At the level of block transfer we do not want to be concerned with the details of the device – the block transfer routines should be much the same whether the device is a small Winchester or a large SMD (semiconductive memory device) drive. The device-dependent details are encapsulated in the *device-driver* software, which is called by the physical I/O routines to perform a transfer. Like the BIOS in CP/M, it presents a hardware-independent interface to the rest of the system.

6.1.2 Physical disc storage

A disc surface is physically formatted into addressable *tracks*, which may also be subdivided into addressable *sectors*. In a multi-surface disc platter, typically found on mainframes, the reading and writing heads move together, so that with the heads positioned on a particular track we can read the corresponding track on all the surfaces. This collection of tracks that can be read without head movement is called a *cylinder*, and disc addressing is usually arranged so that consecutive addresses go through the tracks in one cylinder and then on to the next cylinder. Externally, a disc address is usually of the form cylinder number/track number.

The disc is thus an 'addressable device'. By contrast, a magnetic tape is a non-addressable serial device – the only available operation is to read or write at the point currently reached on the tape. Magnetic tape hardware allows blocks of variable length to be written, but if tapes are used for information transfer or archiving a useful simplification is for the operating system always to write (and subsequently read) information in fixed size blocks the same size as the disc blocks. The rest of the software can then treat discs and tapes as almost identical block devices, except that random access is imposssible on tape.

6.2   DEVICE-LEVEL I/O

The aim of the device-level I/O system is to encapsulate all the device-dependent features of a particular class of peripheral devices, thus presenting a uniform interface to the higher levels of software. The program that controls a device or group of similar devices is called the *device-driver* and runs as a process, synchronized to the device by the interrupt signal(s), and to the 'user' process by a semaphore. Since a device-driver may control a group of devices, there is not a one-to-one correspondence between devices and drivers. However, each device has a unique *device control block* (DCB) associated with it. In order to separate the details of a specific I/O transfer from the generic properties of a device, we use an *I/O transfer request block* (IOTRB) to hold the details of the transfer. A device will in general have a queue of IOTRBs.

The device-driver stands between the requesting process and the peripheral device, and is synchronized using two semaphores. The *device semaphore*, which is essentially the interrupt signal, synchronizes the actual device. (Note that many devices generate more than one kind of interrupt, so the semaphore is logically distinct from the interrupt.) Synchronization with the 'user process' is provided by the *request semaphore*. The device semaphore forms part of the DCB; the request semaphore belongs to the calling process, and is accessed via a pointer held in the IOTRB.

The structure of the DCB and IOTRB is shown in Fig. 6.1. The status report field in the IOTRB allows the device-driver to report errors or anomalies in the transfer. The precise contents of this field will depend on the device.

6.2.1   Device-level disc I/O in a process architecture

We first describe the operation of a disc in a generalized process architecture. There is a queue of requests to be served by the device-driver; new requests are added to the end of the queue, and as requests are serviced their IOTRBs are removed from the queue. Since the queue may become empty we need another semaphore, the *request pending semaphore*, to control the device-driver. Since the queue is a shared resource, access to it must be on an exclusive basis, and so it is protected by yet another semaphore, the *queue semaphore*.

To effect an I/O transfer the calling process constructs an IOTRB (including a local semaphore to act as the busy semaphore), WAITs on the queue semaphore, adds the IOTRB to the device-driver's chain and SIGNALs the queue semaphore (to release the exclusion) and the request pending semaphore (in case the device-driver is halted because the

— chain to next DCB

— pointer to device-driver

— address of interrupt vector

— device specific information

— device semaphore

— head of IOTRB chain

(a)

— buffer address

— number of bytes to transfer

— device address (addressable device only)

— status report

— request semaphore

— process-id of requesting process

— chain to next IOTRB

(b)

Fig. 6.1   Structure of (a) device control block, (b) I/O transfer request block.

queue is empty). The calling process may continue, or may immediately halt by WAITing on its local semaphore. The device-driver executes a cyclic operation as follows. First it performs a WAIT on the queue semaphore: this will halt it if the queue is empty. It then takes an IOTRB from the head of the queue and processes it returning to WAIT on the queue semaphore and repeat the sequence. For simple devices transfers are performed in the order that they appear on the queue. However, a strictly sequential processing may be inefficient. For example, it may be more efficient to order transfers to and from a disc in such a way that all transfers to one cylinder are performed in sequence, and so that the cylinders are examined in sequence. In this way head-movement will be minimized. If the hardware also provides rotational position sensing it may be possible to gain even more by ordering the transfers to minimize rotational latency as well.

6.2.2   Device-level disc I/O in an in-process architecture

Control of discs is less straightforward in an in-process architecture. It will be recalled that in such an architecture all the system software appears in every virtual machine, and services that are shared by several virtual machines are provided by an out-of-process subsystem. On this basis the disc driver should be out-of-process. However, this is only practicable if the overheads of a process-switch are small, since most programs make frequent calls on the disc driver. Since an in-process architecture does not lead to a large number of process switches in the normal way, some such systems do not optimize process switching overheads, and so find the out-of-process solution unacceptable. We cannot just put everything in-process because the device-driver and queue would then appear in all the virtual machines. The queue can be protected by a semaphore as before, but difficulties arise in ensuring that if a virtual machine has started its device-driver, the copies of that same device-driver in the other virtual machines are not activated until the current transfer has finished. Also the sharing of the queue precludes any optimization by reordering the queue of requests. The solution adopted by systems that take this route is to build the device-driver and queue into the kernel and to provide a special locking mechanism to ensure that only one virtual machine can activate its device-driver at any one time. This gives the effect of an out-of-process implementation, without the overheads of the process-switching.

6.3   PHYSICAL LEVEL I/O FOR DISCS

Physical level I/O is just a matter of constructing IOTRBs and passing them to the device-level I/O, then dealing with error situations if they arise. Thus the physical level I/O provides an interface beneath which the device-dependence is concealed.

6.4   LOGICAL I/O FOR DISCS

The function of the logical I/O software is to map a more convenient logical file structure on to the physical disc structure. This logical file structure will usually include files whose size can increase as the program runs. An additional benefit that can be provided at this level is device independence, since it is possible to have the same logical file structure implemented on the basis of two quite different physical disc types. This allows a program to run unchanged on varying hardware configurations.

There are two rather different approaches to mapping the logical file structure on to the physical discs. These can be characterized as the data-processing file approach and the filestore approach. We discuss each of these in turn.

6.4.1 **Data-processing files**

The logical structure presented in this kind of system is one of *files* made up of varying numbers of *records*, all of which are the same size in any one file. The user declares the record size when he creates the file (using a system call). It is assumed that the user may wish to access the records sequentially, or may wish to access individual records identified by a *key*. He therefore also specifies the access method that is to be used, at the time the file is created. Software is provided within the operating system for the various modes of file access. The software for record access and the file structure are obviously related, and with the disregard for precise language that we see all too often in the jargon of computing, the term 'access method' has come to be used for the whole software complex. In older systems all of these access methods were included within the operating system, so that the code could be shared between users. In modern operating systems where code sharing takes place as a matter of course, much of the access method can be regarded a 'library' software to be loaded (notionally) into the user's address space at link-edit time. Either way, it is executed as part of the user process in user-context.

The logical I/O routines call the physical level I/O procedures, and these in turn activate the device-level I/O when required. Since the top level of the access method may wish to wait for completion of the physical operation, we require another semaphore to synchronize the access method and the user program. This is not the same as the busy semaphore which will be used by the access method to synchronize the transfers involved in accessing the desired records.

There are many access methods, and the reader is referred to other texts for full details. Two of the most commonly used are ISAM (Index-Sequential Access Methods) and VSAM (Virtual Sequential Access Method), and we describe these very briefly.

(*i*) *ISAM*
Each record in the file has a key. Records are grouped on to physical tracks (we assume that a track will hold more than one record), and are stored in key-sequential order initially. One track on each cylinder contains an index for the records stored on that cylinder, the index holding the highest record key for each track in the cylinder. A cylinder index records the highest record key in each cylinder, and a pointer to the track index for that cylinder. A *master*

index holds the highest record key in each track of the cylinder index. Thus to access a record the indices are used in sequence, comparing the desired record key with the index entries. The master index identifies a track in the cylinder index, which in turn locates the track index. This index locates the track and thus the record is found. Problems arise when records are added to the file, since the access depends on the ordering of the indices. When an ISAM file is first set up it is usual to leave some empty space in each track for additions, but this merely postpones the evil day: eventually we have to cope with the problem of *overflow*. To cater for this eventuality an overflow area is provided in each cylinder, and the track index has an extra entry pointing to this area. Overflow complicates the access to records, requiring special action, and if there are many overflow records, access can be severely slowed down. For this reason, ISAM files are periodically 'spring-cleaned' and reconstructed at a time when the system is lightly loaded.

(ii) VSAM
VSAM is a recent development of ISAM. Records are stored sequentially as before, with a multi-level index. However, this index takes the form of a B-tree. This provides rapid access and also removes many of the problems of overflow, since the well-known techniques of B-tree organization allow items to be inserted without slowing down search times.

(iii) Other access methods
These include sequential access and *direct access*. This latter method uses hashing to map keys on to disc tracks. The techniques for overflow are similar to those used in hash tables.

6.4.2 Filestores

A rather different kind of data management is found in single-user systems and in multi-access time-sharing systems. In these systems the *filestore* (or filing system) gives each user the ability to store and later retrieve chunks of information (*files*) identified by symbolic name, without any concern for the details of the method of storage. Files can be of two kinds, *text* (character) files and *executable* (binary) files. Some older systems make a rigid distinction between the two sorts of file, but the modern trend is not to emphasize the difference. A method is provided whereby the user of a file can determine whether or not it is an executable file, but to the file system files are just sequences of bytes, whose interpretation is up to the file-user, not the file system. An important characteristic of files is that they are normally accessed sequentially, so there is no need for elaborate access methods. Another important characteristic is that they are of unpredictable and often varying length – every time we edit a text file we change its length. (Well, nearly every time.)

The logical level I/O thus has to map variable-length files with symbolic names on to fixed size tracks (or *blocks* as we shall call them from now on), identified by numerical addresses. Mapping variable length items on to fixed size units is a classical programming problem solved by *chaining*. A simple solution is to use two bytes in each block as a *link* to identify its successor. (Remember that files are accessed sequentially, so simple forward chains are adequate.) Unused blocks are collected on a free chain: blocks are taken from this chain to create or extend a file, and when a file is deleted its blocks can be returned to the free chain for reuse. With this organization a file is uniquely identified if we know the block-number of its first block, so the remaining part of the logical I/O is a mapping between symbolic names and block numbers. This is the province of the *file directory*. Each user has a directory which contains one entry for each of his files. Although the primary purpose of the directory is to map the file name on to a block number, the directory entry will usually contain further information. A typical file-directory entry is shown in Fig. 6.2.

In a multi-user system there will be one file directory per user, so

file name

block number of initial block

access control
   (write permission)

housekeeping:

   typically date/time of
   creation, and date/time of
   last access, and length of
   file (in blocks)

Fig. 6.2   Contents of file directory entry.

there must also be a *master file directory*, indexed by user-id, to give the location of the user directory. The directory system is thus a two-level tree (as illustrated in Fig. 6.3), and a file is identified by a composite name consisting of the user-id and the file name. In most systems the user-id provided at log-in is assumed as a default, being automatically prefixed to any unadorned file name. Thus a full file name (including user-id) is used only when accessing a file in another user's directory.

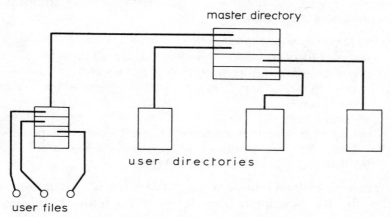

Fig. 6.3 Simple directory structure.

In some systems the directories are built into the operating system in an intimate manner. There is, however, much to be gained by taking the view that directories are just files, like any other files except that only the operating system can write to them. The advantage is that if directories are special, then every operation on them requires special software, whereas if they are regarded as files, most of the manipulations on directories can be accomplished using file-handling software that exists already.

6.4.3 File I/O

We now outline the operations involved in file I/O. We assume that the file exists: file creation will be discussed later. Since a file consists of fixed size blocks, we will need a buffer between the file and the user program. At any time, one of the blocks of the file will be in the buffer, and reading/writing will be taking place at a particular byte address within the buffer. Thus to access a file we need to know the following:

Current block number
Buffer address
Position within buffer

We also need to keep a record of the length of the file while it is open for writing. This information is gathered into a *file control block* (*FCB*), cometimes called a *file descriptor*.

Before a file can be used it must be opened by a call to a system procedure, giving the file name as an argument. The action of the open procedure is as follows:

open(file-name, access-mode)
    use user-id provided at log-in to locate directory in MFD
    check file exists in directory, error if not present
    check requested access-mode against permissions, error if
        no match
    allocate a buffer
    set up FCB with buffer address, current block = 1, position in
        buffer = 0, and length of file as given in directory
    if read access, read first block to buffer

The open procedure returns a *file-identifier* (*file-id*), an integer that locates the file descriptor. This file-id is used for all subsequent accesses to the file.

Once the file is opened, we can read or write the file. These operations are again carried out by procedures that define the physical-level I/O as follows.

read(file-id, memory-address, count)
    {transfers *count* bytes to memory starting at specified address}
    abort if file length zero
    use file-id to locate FCB
    move bytes from buffer to memory, updating position field in FCB
    if end of buffer reached before count expires, and not end-of-file,
        read next block to buffer (using device level I/O)
    if end-of-file, abort with suitable return code
    (Typically the return code is a count of bytes transferred, negative
        value indicating error)

write(file-id, memory-address, count)
    {transfers *count* bytes from memory to file, starting at address
        indicated}
    use file-id to locate FCB
    transfer bytes to buffer, updating position field in FCB
    if end of buffer reached before count expires, write buffer to disc;

> obtain new block from free chain and enter its number in FCB
> increment length count in FCB

Finally, a file must be closed. Apart from tidying up, if the file was open for writing it is necessary to flush out the buffer to write the last block to disc.

close(file-id)
> use file-id to locate FCB
> if open for writing, write buffer to disc with 'end of file' link
> return buffer and FCB to pool

The astute reader will have noticed that we have made no provision for updating the housekeeping information in the directory (details of last access and current length). One way of fixing this omission is for the 'open' procedures to record the file name in the FCB so that 'close' can use this to find the directory and update it. A better solution is presented later.

Creating and removing files

Creating a file is just a matter of creating a directory entry with the file-length set to zero. Actual space for the file will be acquired as a side-effect of the 'write' calls. A system procedure is provided:

createfile(file_name, access_permissions)

Removing a file is achieved by a similar system call which deletes the directory entry and returns the disc blocks to the free chain.

6.4.4 More about directories

The two-level directory structure is the simplest we can get away with. There are many advantages in having a hierarchical directory structure, in which each directory entry can point to a file or to another directory. (Fig. 6.4.) One advantage of this organization is that the directory structure can reflect the management structure of the organization. However, a hierarchical directory system is equally useful for individual users, since it allows a user to group logically related files in a single directory, e.g. all source code in one directory, executable programs in another and documentation in a third. Keeping one's files in a structured manner is beneficial in the same way as structured programming is.

At first sight, multiple-level directories complicate the file system housekeeping. A great simplification can be achieved by observing that the housekeeping information is a property of the *file*, and is quite

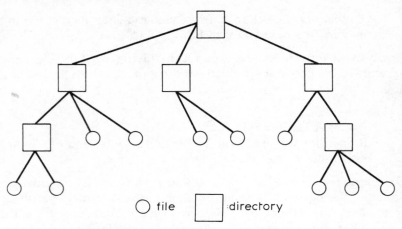

Fig. 6.4   Hierarchical directory system.

independent of the method used to name the file. A tree-structured directory gives us a more elaborate mapping between the file name and the file, and it is only when we have identified the file that we need to access the housekeeping information. We thus need a data structure to contain this information; this structure then becomes an abstration of the file, and the function of the directory is to map from a symbolic name to this structure. In UNIX the structure is called (for irrelevant historical reasons) an *i-node*. The i-node contains the disc address of the file, the access permissions, the length and the related housekeeping information (date/time of last access, etc.). The i-nodes are collected into an array, and so a file can be represented internally by a single number, the *i-number*, which indexes the array to select an i-node. Since directories are themselves files, the directory tree contains only names and i-numbers. The structure of the UNIX filing system is illustrated in Fig. 6.5. Since the housekeeping information is held in the i-node, not in the directory, the file-closing problem alluded to earlier now disappears. The file-id of the earlier exposition is the same as the i-number, and this is all we need on a file-close – we don't need to know the symbolic name of the file in order to do the necessary tidying up.

It is interesting to note that separating the file from its name in this way enables us to superimpose a hierarchical directory system on *any* file system: the difference is that at the bottom level the directories map on to file-names in the host system, rather than i-numbers of files. This is the basis of the 'Portable File Directory System' that has been implemented on a number of computer systems.

In a multi-level directory system a file is identified by a sequence of names that trace a path throught the tree, all except the last name in the

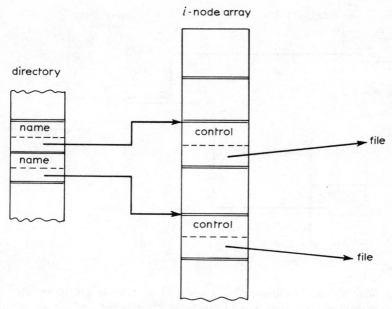

Fig. 6.5 UNIX filing system.

sequence being directory names. Such a name is often called a *path name*: in UNIX the path name consists of the component names separated by strokes. The root directory has '/' as its name, so a typical UNIX path name might be '/usr/csg/dwb/osbook/chapter5'. Such a naming system is cumbersome, and it is usual to incorporate the concept of a *current directory*, whose identification (itself a path name) is prefixed to any path name that does not begin with a stroke (in the same way as the full name of a file in a simple system consists of the concatenation of the user name and the file name). Thus if the current directory is set to '/usr/csg/dwb/osbook' a reference to 'chapter5' as a file name will generate the full path name given in the example above. In UNIX each user has a 'home directory' which is set as his current directory when he logs in; subsequently he can change the current directory by an explicit command. Each directory includes a reference to its parent under the name '. .', so it is possible to move up and down the directory tree at will (subject to access permission being granted by the owners of the directories).

The isolation of the mapping function of the directories from the files themselves opens the way to *'file aliasing'*, since more than one path name can map on to the same i-node (Fig. 6.6). At first sight this seems a dangerous and not very useful facility, but it does in fact have some

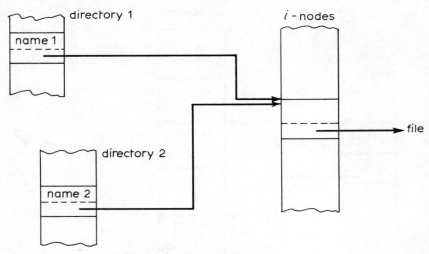

Fig. 6.6 File aliasing.

practical value. For example, a user may have a group of files with descriptive names, e.g. 'stock', 'orders', 'prices' etc., while for certain of his programs it would be more convenient if the files had systematic names, e.g. F0, F1, F2, etc. Aliasing solves this problem. Another use of aliasing commonly found in UNIX systems is to create abbreviations for frequently used long path-names. However, the general rule of programming that names should identify objects uniquely within a given context is not lightly to be cast aside, and aliases should be used with discretion.

6.4.5 File sharing

An important feature of a multi-user time-sharing system is the ability to share files. If this can be done simply and conveniently it enhances individual productivity by allowing generally useful programs and data to be disseminated amongst the user community. It also eases the task of the system administrator, since new compilers and utilities can be made available to all users as shareable files, without the need to take special steps to incorporate them in the operating system. File sharing is not the same as file aliasing: a shared file has a unique path name, whereas an aliased file is identified by two or more path names.

File sharing can be organized on an individual or a group basis. In either case a file has a unique *owner* (whose identity is recorded in the *i*-node or the directory), and the owner has control over the sharing (if any) allowed for his file. Individual sharing implies that the owner can designate specific users to have access to a file: group sharing means that the owner can extend access only to certain groups of users. Individual sharing tends to lead to complicated directory structures, and modern systems usually limit sharing to group sharing. We now describe two typical file-sharing mechanisms, those of UNIX and DEC's RSTS.

In RSTS the user-id is in two parts, a *project number* and a *programmer number*, e.g. [136,7]. The full name of a file consists of the owner's id prefixed to the file name, e.g. '[136,7]DATA.DAT'; if the user-id is omitted it is assumed to be the id provided at log-in in the usual way. For file-sharing purposes the world is divided into three disjoint subsets:

(1) The owner,
(2) Users with the same project number as the owner,
(3) Users with a different project number.

These subsets define the groups for file-sharing purposes. Each file has a 6-bit protection code in which the bits provided independent read-and-write protection against the three groups. Setting a bit in the protection code stops the appropriate (read or write) access for a particular group. Thus it is possible for a user to allow other members of the same project group access to a file, while preventing access by users outside the project group. Public files can be given general read permission by not setting any of the read-protection bits. At the other extreme a user can set write-protection against himself – possibly useful for a vital file that must not be accidentally edited. (It is even possible for a user to set read-protection against himself, though it is difficult to envisage the circumstances in which this would be useful.) This protection mechanism applies to data files: for executable files the user can specify read-and-write protection or execute protection against each of the groups. This allows utilities to be made available for general use as executable files, without the ability for the users to read or change them.

The UNIX system is not dissimilar. Users are allocated to groups by the system manager, and the categories recognized by the protection system are:

(1) The file owner,
(2) The owner's group,
(3) Everybody.

UNIX specifies who *may* access a file, rather than specifying prohibitions as in RSTS. For each of the three categories, individual read, write and execute permissions can be specified. The protection code (or 'mode') of a file is thus a 9-bit quantity, but it is customary to write it as a 9-character sequence using the letters r, w, x to indicate read, write and execute permission repectively, and a dash to indicate no permissions.

Permissions are listed in the sequence owner, group, everyone, thus 'rw-r- -r- -' would indicate read and write permission for the owner, and read permission for everyone else. A system utility might have permissions 'rwx- -x- -x' indicating that anyone can execute the file, but only the owner can read or write it. A very private file might be given permission 'r- - - - - - - -', i.e. the only access is reading by the owner. The permissions have a slightly different meaning when applied to directory files. Write permission for a directory implies the ability to delete files contained therein, while execute permission implies ability to search the directory. Thus a permission 'rwx-r-xr-x' would give general access to the directory, but restrict deletion to the owner of the directory. 'rwx- -x- -x' would allow other users to search the directory but not to read it. Thus a user could use a path-name that included this directory, but he would not be able to inspect the directory. This technique can be used to make selected items of system software available to users while maintaining the privacy of the system directories. 'rwx- - - - - -' stops anyone but the owner searching the directory, and thus effectively blocks off everything in the hierarchy below this directory. With careful setting of permissions it is thus possible to achieve close control over file access.

6.4.6. Disc organization

We have so far assumed that there is only one disc, but this will rarely be the case. In a mainframe system with many discs, file-placement is determined by the system administrator who allocates users to particular discs. This allocation is recorded in the system so that when a file is created the appropriate disc can be chosen, and the disc identity can be recorded in the directory to permit future access to the file. Minicomputer systems often have a small number of disc drives with demountable disc packs, so that the total collection of user files may extend over more discs than can be actually on-line at a particular time. In systems for this environment it is usual for each disc-pack to hold a self-contained file system complete with a master directory. Again, UNIX and DEC systems illustrate two different approaches.

In DEC systems the disc contains files for a number of users. The master directory is indexed by a user-id (of the form [project number, programmer number]), and gives the location of the directory for that user's files. The full hierarchical name for a file is thus a concatenation of disc-identifier, user identifier and file name, e.g. 'RL1:[136,7]DATA.DAT'. Given such a file name the system will access disc RL1, scan the master directory for [136,7] to locate the user's directory, then locate the user's file. For most file accesses only the file name need be given, the disc and user being determined by default: only when accessing another user's files or a system library is the full file identify required.

The DEC system makes the disc identity explicit. UNIX offers a similar facility for demountable file systems, but the disc identity is absorbed into the directory hierarchy, and so is transparent to the user. As with the DEC system, each demountable disc holds a self-contained file-system with a *root directory* which is the root of the typical tree-structured hierarchy of directories and files. UNIX allows such a file system to be *mounted* at a node in an existing file system. The combined file system thus has a tree structure with one or more subtrees held on separate demountable discs. The existence of the demountable discs is, however, totally invisible to the user. For example, suppose that a library of files is held on a disc pack. To make this available to users it is first necessary to establish a dummy directory called 'lib' (the name is arbitrary) in the top level directory (see Fig. 6.7(a)).

If the library disc is loaded on device RL2 (say), the command

> mount   /dev/rl2   /usr/lib

causes the file system to treat any path-name starting /usr/lib specially: /usr/lib is treated as a synonym for the (anonymous) root directory of the file system 'mounted on /urs/lib'. Thus to the user there is still a hierarchical file system, as illustrated in Fig. 6.7(b).

When the disc is to be unloaded, the command

> umount   /dev/rl2

breaks the connection, and /usr/lib reverts to being a dummy directory. (Note that /dev/rl2 is the UNIX way of referring to device RL2: the significance of this form of identification will become apparent later.)

This mechanism very conveniently allows 'personal' file archives on floppy disc to be made accessible within the normal file system. The user sets up a dummy directory 'rx0' in his directory, and mounting the floppy disc drive on this directory makes 'rx0' a synonym for the root directory of the file system on the floppy. A file called 'foo' on the floppy is accessed as 'rx0/foo'. Thus an apparently uniform file system can be constructed, spread over a diversity of devices.

6.4.7 Some variations

Most filestores conform broadly to the pattern just described. In this section we describe significant variations that are found in some systems.

(a) Detached chains

The file structure as described is a chained structure, with each block

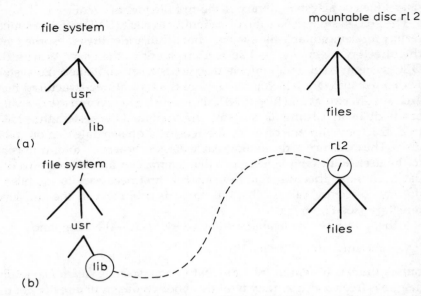

Fig. 6.7 (a) File system before mounting /dev/rl2, (b) file store after mounting file system from /dev/rl2.

holding the disc address of its successor (or an end-of-file indication). An alternative is to store the chains in an array, so that chain [*n*] contains the address of the successor to block *n*. The disadvantage of detached chains is that by gathering all the 'control' information into a contiguous area of the disc we increase the vulnerability of the file system, since a failure to read this area of the disc effectively loses the whole file system. This eventuality is particularly likely to occur in floppy-disc-based systems, where the in-contact reading heads cause wear on the disc. If a chain area has to be read very frequently, it is much more likely to suffer damage leading to mis-reads.

A particularly simple version of detached chains is found in CP/M. In this system the floppy disc is divided into *extents* each occupying a (fixed) number of tracks, and a file occupies an integral number of extents. Small files, which are quite common, fit into one extent, and the directory entry identifies this extent. If a file occupies more than one extent it has a corresponding number of file-directory entries; an extra field in the directory gives the extent number. Thus the extent is the unit of disc allocation, and the extents are chained together in the directory.

UNIX (as might be expected) has a novel disc organization which is a form of detached chaining. The i-node contains a *map* giving the disc blocks occupied by the file. (Blocks are obtained from a free list also organized as a map, as required.) The map consists of thirteen addresses. The first ten of these hold the block numbers of the first ten blocks of the file. For large files, the eleventh address points to a block that contains the block numbers of the next 128 blocks of the file. (This is called an indirect block.) For still larger files, the twelfth address points to up to 128 blocks, each of which points to 128 blocks of the file (a 'double indirect' block). Gigantic files use the thirteenth address as a 'triple-indirect' block. This organization is geared to the observation that in the UNIX environment many files are small, but some files are very large. It gives rapid access to small files while allowing files of over a thousand million bytes. An incidental advantage is that it gives a form of direct access that is reasonably efficient in the first ten blocks of a file.

(b) Backward chains

The loss of chaining imformation is particularly infuriating, since the contents of the files are still on the disc, but totally inaccessible. As noted, floppy-disc systems are particularly prone to this kind of loss. The Apple LISA protects the user against this possibility by recording in each block the identity of the file to which the block belongs, and its sequence number in the file. Thus a damaged file system can be reconstructed. The overheads in space occupied on the disc are substantial, and the technique in possible only because the LISA has novel hardware which allows an unusually large amount of information to be recorded on a floppy disc.

(c) Hash-coded filestores

An alternative way of protecting against loss of the directory is not to have a directory on the disc at all. This novel approach was used in an experimental system built at the University of Strathclyde. The disc is divided into *logical tracks* each consisting of a number of consecutive physical sectors. Typically, a logical track might consist of two 128-byte sectors on a floppy disc, or eight 512-byte sectors on a hard disc when most files are large. An area at the start of each logical track is reserved for system use and contains the 'logical track name'. If the logical track is not part of a file it has the name 'system:free', and if it contains one or more physical tracks that cannot be read it has the name 'system:bad'. (This makes it possible to avoid a damaged area on the disc.) If the logical track is holding part of a file its logical track name is formed by concatenating the file name with the sequence number of this track within the file. The file store is organized in exactly the same way as a hash table. To access a file the software first forms the logical track name of the desired track and uses this as an input to a hash function to obtain a first possible logical track number. (The hash function maps logical track names on to integers in the range 1 to n, where n is the number of logical tracks on the disc. The mapping need not be unique, but should generate values fairly evenly spread over the range $1. . .n$.) The name of the selected track is compared with the desired logical track name, and if they do not match the succeeding logical tracks are searched in ascending order of addresses until either a match is obtained or a free track is encountered. This latter eventuality means that the desired logical track name does not exist on the disc. There is no directory; every time the file is accessed the hashing procedure is followed. Performance is greatly improved by using a cache which, like the paging translation buffer, records the names of the logical tracks recently accessed, together with their actual disc addresses.

6.4.8   Recovery from hardware failures

An important requirement of a filing system is that the user should have confidence that files stored therein will still be there when required at some indeterminate future time. Although modern computing equipment is very reliable, discs are subject to failure and the filing system must provide some capability to recover from such failures. Excluding castastrophic failure of the drive, there are two common errors:

(1) Bad read: one or more tracks on the disc cannot be read. At best, this causes loss of part of a file; at worst it may cause loss of a directory or other system information such as the i-nodes. Floppy discs are particularly prone to this kind of error when the disc or the head is worn.

(2) Rogue write: information is successfully written, but on the wrong track. If chains are held in the disc blocks, this will corrupt the chains so that part of one file apparently overwrites another file. A nasty variant of this error is a bad write that links a file in use to the free block chain. This is particularly insidious, since the chaos rapidly spreads through the file system. (This is of course an argument in favour of detached chains.)

These errors are hardware errors; some systems are liable to another form of disc corruption arising from the software. In order to improve the efficiency of disc access, some systems use a 'software cache'. Blocks that are to be written to the disc are first placed in the cache, and only later written to the disc. This means that if a block is being updated frequently, it will be found in the cache, and it will not be necessary to read it from the disc repeatedly. However, any fault which causes the processor to stop (e.g. power failure) will leave the disc in an inconsistent state, and any files that were being accessed just before the fault are liable to be corrupted.

We thus need to be able to recover from these malfunctions with as little loss of information as possible. Recovery is only possible in the worst case if up-to-date duplicate copies of files and directories are available. In designing a recovery system, a number of factors have to be balanced:

(1) What is the mean time between failure (MTBF) of the disc hardware? This will have a bearing on the frequency with which copies should be made.
(2) What is the operational cost of making the copies? If the copying requires the cessation of normal operation this may not be acceptable.
(3) What is the cost to the organization of loss of information? Loss of the current version of a program under development may not be critical: loss of information in a banking organization, for example, would be catastrophic.

100% protection requires that everything is recorded in duplicate (or even triplicate): this is expensive in hardware, and we look at less drastic strategies appropriate to organizations where some degree of data loss can be tolerated. The simplest technique is the *massive dump* in which the entire file system is copied on to another medium (usually magnetic tape). This takes time (several hours for a large file system) during which the computer system cannot be used. It is therefore appropriate if the MTBF is large, so that infrequent dumps are adequate, and if the consequences of data loss are not critical. For example, if the massive dump is done during the night to avoid interfering with normal work, up to one day's work can be lost if it is necessary to 'back-up' the file system to recover from a disc crash.

A technique that meets most requirements is the *incremental dump*. Dumps are made at regular (frequent) intervals, but only those files that have changed since the last dump are actually copied to tape. The incremental dump thus provides an 'audit trail' of filestore transactions from which the state of the filestore can be restored to that holding at the time of the most recent dump. Thus only work done since the last dump is lost, and if dumps are frequent this loss can be minimized. Incremental dumping can take place in parallel with normal operation: the only restriction is that a particular user cannot write to his files while they are being dumped. The slight hiccup that this causes is unlikely to be noticed.

The incremental dump requires that the system record the date and time whenever a file is updated, as well as the date and time of creation of a new file. (Creation or deletion of files involves writing to the directory, and the same mechanism will record the date and time of this change.) To start the incremental dump cycle a massive dump of the entire file system is taken: this defines an origin for the audit trail. The dump program is then run at an interval T (which may be measured in minutes, hours or days), generating a sequence of dump tapes 1. . .N, constructed as follows. (We use UNIX terminology in the description, though the technique is applicable to any system.) The file system is explored systematically, starting at the root directory. Each file (directory) is checked, and if it was created, or has been updated since the (known) time of last dump, it is recorded on the dump tape. (In UNIX the control information for the file is held in the i-node, so this must also be dumped. In other systems the control information is held in the directory. In this case, updating the file will change the directory, and so it will automatically get dumped. In either case, creation or deletion of a file modifies the directory and causes it to be dumped. Thus files and directories remain consistent on the dump tape.) This process is continued until all files (directories) have been examined.

In the event of a disc crash the recovery process is as follows. Let the most recent dump tape be denoted as tape N, its predecessor as tape $N-1$, etc. Tape N is loaded and the files are extracted; in the process the directories or i-nodes are updated to reflect the new locations of the files on the disc. We now have a partial file-system, containing all the files that were created or updated since the previous dump, and every directory that refers to a new or changed file. Tape N-1 is now loaded, and is first scanned for directories. If a directory on this tape is also present on the disc it can be ignored, since it is superseded by the later dump, otherwise it is put on the disc, and its parent directory updated to record its new position. Then we look at the files on the tape. There are three possibilities:

(1) The file is already on the disc; that copy is the most recent one and the tape copy can be discarded.
(2) The file is not on the disc but is referenced in a directory on the disc. In this case the file was unchanged between dumps and should be restored to the disc, updating the directory to record its new position.
(3) The file is not on the disc, and is not referenced in a directory on the disc. This file was deleted between dumps $N-1$ and N, and so can be ignored.

The same process is repeated with tapes $N-2$, $N-3$ . . . until the complete file system has been rebuilt. This rebuilding can proceed in parallel with normal use of the system, except that users may be held up if they try to access a file that has not yet been restored.

The only files lost are those created or changed since the last dump before the incident. The loss can clearly be minimized by increasing the dump frequency, and the system administrator must choose this in the light of the considerations described above. Incremental dumping at frequent intervals creates a lot of dump tapes, and the sheer logistics of handling a large number of tapes will slow down the recovery process. It is therefore common practice to combine frequent incremental dumps with a periodic massive dump to establish a new origin. If this is not feasible, it may be desirable to compact the dump tapes by removing from earlier tapes files that have later been changed or deleted. The process is very similar to the recovery process already outlined.

7
Terminals, printers and networks

7.1 CHARACTER DEVICES

VDUs and printers are almost universal as the terminal devices for multi-user time-shared systems, and the keyboard and monitor of the personal computer play the same roles as a VDU (visual display unit). We describe these as *character-serial* devices because the character is the unit of information transfer, and characters are transmitted in sequence between computer and device. (Note that this excludes the kind of I/O commonly used in home computers. In many such machines the display is *memory mapped*, and the keyboard is organized as a matrix. For input, the keyboard is scanned periodically to determine the row and column corresponding to a key that has been pressed. For output an area of memory is assigned as the screen map, containing one byte for each pixel position on the screen. A special chip scans this area of memory continuously and displays the appropriate symbols. Output to the screen thus requires merely that the program write to the appropriate place in the map.) Terminal I/O is organized broadly in the same manner as disc I/O, the software being divided into device-level, physical and logical levels. Even in a single-user system this division is necessary. At device level a program has to know the addresses assigned to the I/O chip, and the correct sequence of control signals to be sent to achieve the desired operation. This kind of detail is highly hardware-dependent, and needs to be hidden from the higher levels of operating system software. In a multi-user system there is additional complication at the device level since many terminals are usually multiplexed on to one physical interface. At the physical level the software has to deal with echoing of input characters, and the recognition of special control sequences in the input; it may also have to implement flow-control if information is being produced faster than the user (or printer) can absorb it. At the logical level it is usually convenient to have facilities for correcting typing mistakes 'on the fly', and for simulating features that a particular terminal might not have built-in, such as tabs.

7.2   THE TERMINAL INTERFACE IN CP/M

To illustrate some of the problems and techniques, we first describe how CP/M handles terminal input–output, and before we can do this we need to digress slightly and explain the form of CP/M *system calls*.

In CP/M all the hardware-dependent code is gathered into BIOS, and BDOS presents a hardware-independent interface to the user. To access BDOS facilities the program must place in the C register the number of the system call required, and then make a subroutine jump to a fixed location in BDOS (usually address 005H). BDOS then transfers control to the appropriate address in BIOS. In this way the interface remains the same even though the address of the appropriate BIOS function may change. For convenience the relevant CP/M system calls are listed in Table 7.1.

Table 7.1   Some CP/M system calls

1 Console input
2 Console output
3 Reader input
4 Punch output
5 List output
6 Direct console I/O
9 Print string
10 Read console buffer
11 Get console status

The most fundamental operation is direct console I/O (system call 6). This transfers one character to or from the console in a transparent manner (i.e. without ascribing special meaning to control characters). If the E register contains any byte other than FF that character is sent to the display. If the E register contains FF the system will wait for a key to be depressed and place the code for that key in the A register without any attempt to interpret it. Of course, if no key is pressed the system will just wait indefinitely. To obviate this system call 11 (get console status) can be used. This returns FF in register A if a key has been pressed and the character not read, and returns zero otherwise.

These two system calls correspond to the device-level in our layered I/O, and will rarely be used except by sophisticated users. Most users require something more. At the very least they will want characters from the keyboard echoed to the screen. The next level of I/O in CP/M (roughly corresponding to the physical level in our model) provides keyboard echo, and certain other useful facilities. Console input (system call 1) reads the next character from the keyboard to the A register. If this is a graphic character (i.e. a printable character) it is echoed to the screen: non-printing characters are not echoed except for return, linefeed, backspace and tab. The first three are echoed as themselves, but a tab character is echoed as a number of spaces, the number being chosen to simulate tab stops at fixed positions across the screen. (This is actually an example of logical I/O – the distinction between logical and physical I/O is not clear-cut in CP/M.) Console output (system call 2) sends the character from the E register to the screen; if it is a tab it is replaced by the appropriate number of spaces. The I/O system at this level also controls two other useful features, printer echo and scroll control. Printer echo allows output sent to the screen to be sent to the printer at the same time, so as to obtain hard copy. Scroll control allows the user to stop output temporarily so that he can read what is on the screen, and to restart it when he is ready to go on. Printer echo is turned on by control-P, and turned off by a subsequent control-P; scrolling is stopped by control-S and restarted by another control-S. The status of these two facilities is recorded internally by flags, and console output checks the flags each time it is called. If printer echo is set ON, the character is sent to the printer as well as the screen. If scrolling is set OFF, then console output will wait for it to be switched ON again before proceeding. If a control-P or control-S is read by console input the appropriate flag will be switched, and another character read from the keyboard. However, it is more likely that these two control combinations will be typed when there is no input request outstanding. (If scrolling has been stopped, the program will be waiting for console output to return control, so cannot possibly read the keyboard.) It is therefore necessary for CP/M to react to these characters in the absence of a console input call, and this is achieved by keeping a one-character buffer between the keyboard and the calling program. When a key is pressed at a time when console input has not been requested, the character is examined: if it is control-S or control-P appropriate action is taken, otherwise the character is placed in the buffer and will be picked up by console input next time it is called.

Most CP/M programmers in fact use a higher level interface provided by system calls 9 (print string) and 10 (read console buffer). Print string is a convenience: given a starting address it takes a sequence of characters from successive bytes in memory and sends them to the screen, stopping when it finds a '$' character. It expands tabs, and takes account of printer echo and scroll on/off, just like console output. Read console buffer provides a logical I/O level that allows for the correction of errors 'on the fly'. The user provides a buffer of up to 256 bytes, and sets the length of the buffer as the value of the first byte. Given the address of the buffer, the system call reads and echoes characters from the keyboard until either the buffer overflows or the line is terminated by 'return' of 'linefeed'. The number of characters read is recorded in the second byte of the buffer. During input, various control characters are recognized and acted upon specially, as follows:

(1) Control-H: backspaces one character position in the buffer, thus erasing the last character typed.
(2) Control-X: backspaces to the start of the line, allowing over-typing.
(3) Control-E: echoes as linefeed, return but doesn't put anything in the buffer – useful for typing lines wider than the screen.
(4) Control-U: discards buffer contents and echoes linefeed, return.
(5) Rub-out: removes and echoes the last character (used on hard-copy terminals only).
(6) Control-R: retypes the current line (used in conjunction with rub-out to print a 'clean' version of a line after correction).
(7) Control-C: at the start of a line causes a 'warm boot', i.e. initialization of CP/M.

7.3   TERMINAL HANDLING IN MULTI-USER SYSTEMS

A multi-user system has to provide a similar interface to that provided by CP/M, to all the users. There are, however, two additional complications. One arises from the process scheduling: terminal I/O must continue independently of whether the process associated with the terminal is running, free or halted – users expect to be able to type at any time. The other complication arises from the fact that economic considerations dictate that several terminal devices are multiplexed on to a single physical I/O port. Decoupling the I/O from the process status means that the terminal handling must be done out-of-process, with suitable buffering to accumulate characters typed while a process is halted. The multiplexing of terminals on to a single interface requires a software demultiplexing in the device-handler.

7.3.1   Handling multiplexed terminals

It is prohibitively expensive to provide a separate interface for every terminal on a multi-user system. Instead, designers take advantage of the fact that terminal I/O is slow – most users type at a speed of a few characters per second, and terminals accept output at speeds between 100 and 1000 characters per second. It is therefore perfectly easy to produce a hardware interface that can monitor several lines at once. Information is transmitted *serially* between terminal and computer, at speeds of up to 9600 bits per second. On input, having seen and attended to a bit from a particular line, there is ample time for the other lines to be scanned before the next bit arrives on the line in question. Thus on input a multiplexer *scans* up to 16 lines in a round-robin manner, assembling characters from the serial bits as they are received. When a complete character has been received the multiplexer delivers a byte-pair: the first byte identifies the terminal that sent the character, and the second byte contains the actual character. Likewise, the multiplexer accepts output in the form of byte-pairs, a terminal identifier and a character to be sent. It cycles round the communication lines sending characters in serial form; as on input, having transmitted one bit on a particular line there is time to attend to the other lines before the next bit needs to be sent on the original line. Typically, a multiplexer handles sixteen terminals.

The device handler for a terminal multiplexer has to present it to the higher levels of software as a number of distinct logical devices. This is achieved by having two buffer arrays, so that there is an input buffer and an output buffer for each terminal. Associated with each buffer is a flag; for an input buffer the flag is set when there is information in the buffer, while for an output buffer the flag indicates that the buffer is free to receive further information. When the multiplexer delivers a byte-pair the first byte identifies the buffer and the device-driver can deposit the character appropriately, setting the flag if necessary. On the output side, the device-driver cycles round the output buffers. Each time it receives an interrupt to signal completion of an output operation it advances to the next non-empty buffer, extracts a character and sends the appropriate byte-pair to the multiplexer. The flags act as semaphores whereby the higher levels of software can synchronize, waiting for input to arrive or waiting for an output buffer to become free. The simplest approach is to make the buffers one line in length, but there is advantage in having longer buffers so that the user can type ahead, and programs need not be halted just because they are trying to output more than one line at a time. This device-driver construction completely conceals the multiplexer from the rest of the system, in accordance with the general design philosophy of hiding aspects of the hardware that are irrelevant to the task in hand.

7.4   TERMINAL I/O IN UNIX

The UNIX terminal driver provides a very flexible interface, and serves as a model to illustrate the design requirements of terminal handling. The device-driver uses the mechanisms already described to conceal the multiplexing from the rest of the system, and provides input and output buffers for each active communication line. However, the buffers are not of fixed size, and are therefore referred to as *queues*. A queue is constructed by chaining together a number of *buffer blocks* each of which holds six characters. Each buffer block contains a pointer to the next, and the queue itself is represented as a block containing a character count and pointers to the head and the tail of the queue. Unused buffer blocks are kept on a free list, and as blocks in a queue are emptied by the I/O processes they are returned to the free list for reuse. Installation dependent parameters determine the maximum number of blocks that can comprise a user's input or output queue. UNIX provides many options, and we shall first consider the 'plain vanilla' input–output that the user gets by default. We shall then describe how the user can tailor the system to his own requirements.

7.4.1 Device-level software

On input, the device-driver accepts characters from the line and adds them to the appropriate queue (known as the *raw* queue, since no processing of the characters is done at this stage) until one of the following characters is seen:

End of line (usually RETURN)
End of file (ASCII EOT, octal code 004)
Rub-out (ASCII DEL, octal code 0177)

or until the 'hang-up' signal (carrier-fail) is received on a modem-driven communications line. Any one of these constitutes a 'break', and causes further processing of the input. End-of-line or end-of-file initiate further processing by the logical I/O level. Rub-out and hang-up cause the queue to be flushed out, and a software interrupt to be sent to the process(es) associated with the terminal. In addition to placing an input character on the raw queue, the device-driver also places the character on the corresponding output queue so as to echo it. Backspace is echoed as 'backspace–space–backspace' to wipe out the character on the screen, and the 'delete-line' character is echoed as a newline. An option exists to suppress echo entirely (useful when reading passwords). As in CP/M, scrolling can be stopped by typing control-S. On receiving this character the device-driver sets a flag for the output routines, but does not place the control-S in the raw queue. If the flag is set, *any* input character will reset it and send a wake-up signal to the output driver (in case no terminals are currently awaiting output). However, a control-Q is never placed in the raw queue, and so this character restarts scrolling if it was stopped, but has no other effect.

The output side of the device-driver scans the output queues for the active terminals, looking for non-empty queues for which output has not been inhibited by a control-S. If no such queues can be found it goes to sleep (and will be awakened when a queue becomes non-empty or a previously inhibited output is freed by an input character). More usually there are characters to output, and the device-driver takes characters from each non-empty queue in turn and sends them to the multiplexer. As an option, tabs can be replaced by the appropriate number of spaces to simulate fixed tab-stops, just as in CP/M. For terminals with a limited character set, the device-driver can also perform translations (e.g. lower-case to upper-case). The translation mechanism is table-driven, and is thus completely general.

7.4.2 The logical I/O system

The terminal interface seen by the user consists of the output queue already discussed and a further input queue called the *cooked* queue (cooked being the next stage from raw). When an end-of-line or end-of-file is received, the logical I/O level is activated to transfer characters from the raw queue to the cooked queue, dealing with backspace and delete-line characters in the process. A backspace causes the character just placed in the cooked queue to be discarded, while a delete-line discards the whole of the cooked queue. As is usual in UNIX, a backslash preceding either of these characters removes the special meaning. The user's interface thus consists of two functions calls, getc and putc. Since characters are moved into the cooked queue only at end-of-line (or file), in a sense input is line oriented; if the cooked queue is empty a getc call will have to wait until an end-of-line is received from the terminal. However, the dynamic nature of the raw queue means that the user can type ahead freely, and does not have to wait for the system to deal with one line before another line can be typed.

7.4.3 Options

The plain vanilla interface described above can be tailored by the user in many ways. Associated with each active terminal is a control block which determines the current options; this can be updated either by a keyboard command or by a program via a system call. The options fall into three groups.

(1) Terminal characteristics: these include the line speed, parity (in both directions), and delays to be inserted after return and tab (to cater for printing terminals).
(2) Keyboard facilities: these include echo on/off, expansion of tabs, selection of erase and kill characters and selection of end-of-line

character. In the earlier discussion we referred to backspace; this is inconvenient on a printing terminal, and so the user can specify his own erase character. (# is a common choice.) Likewise, although the delete-line (kill) character is usually the non-printing control-X, some users prefer a visible kill character (typically @). Terminals differ in the end-of-line mechanisms; some have a large key labelled RETURN which sends a carriage return, while others have a large key labelled NEWLINE which sends a linefeed. The user can specify which option his terminal uses.

(3) Break mode: UNIX normally transfers characters to the cooked queue on receipt of an end-of-line code. This is inconvenient for some interactive programs, and they can set *cbreak* mode, in which every character causes a break, i.e. characters go straight from the raw queue to the cooked queue. Obviously, no erase or kill processing can be done. *raw* mode, if set, is like cbreak with the additional feature that rub-out is not recognized as an interrupt, parity is not checked, and all 8 bits of the character code are transmitted. It is thus the exact analogue of direct console I/O in CP/M.

The options affect various parts of the I/O system. Terminal characteristics are interrogated by the device-driver, as are the echo switch and the tab expansion switch. The device-driver uses the control block information to decide when an end-of-line has been received: if RETURN is so recognized it is echoed as carriage return, linefeed, while if NEWLINE is specified as the line ending a linefeed terminates the line and is echoed as linefeed, carriage return. The erase and kill characters are obtained from the control block whenever characters are to be transferred from the raw queue to the cooked queue. cbreak and raw modes determine when this transfer takes place.

7.5   PRINTERS

In addition to the terminal, the other common output device in an interactive programming environment is the printer. A printer can always be treated as a simple character device, and indeed the CP/M system call for the 'list device' is virtually the same as the system call 'console out', except that the destination is different. However, although some printers (particulary letter-quality printers like the Diablo and Qume daisy-wheel printers) actually operate on a character-by-character basis, most printers incorporate internal buffering for one or more lines, and to obtain the maximum print speed it is necessary to ensure that there is always a line waiting in the buffer, so that as soon as printing of one line has been finished, printing of another line can start.

Also, since printers, being mechanical, consume output at a relatively slow rate, a system like UNIX that maintains a dynamic buffer pool may need to restrict the flow of output from a process to a printer in order to avoid swamping the buffer pool. Thus the device-level software for printer control is not quite like that for terminal output.

Printers and printer interfaces vary considerably. Typically the printer will have a buffer of at least one line capacity, and printing will start on receipt of a specific code (which may be a special code or may be 'return'), or as soon as a full line of information has been received. At some time after printing has started, the buffer becomes free to accept more characters. This is signalled to the driver by setting a bit in the *printer status word*. In addition to this 'ready' bit, the status word usually provides other signals, e.g. 'paper out', 'fault', and may also include an 'interrupt enable' bit. If this bit is set by the driver, then the setting of any of the other bits will generate an interrupt. The overheads of an interrupt for every character sent to a printer are very high, and so when the driver has data for the printer it usually sends it as a block with interrupts inhibited. Strictly, the driver should clear the ready bit, send a character and loop waiting for the ready bit to be set again. However, it is not uncommon for the driver to write characters one after another, on the assumption that the printer can accept them faster than the driver can send them. Once the last character has been sent (which will be a 'start print' signal), interrupts are enabled so that as soon as the printer is free it can be sent more characters (if there are any waiting.)

We can now follow the sequence of events as a program sends data to the printer. We use UNIX as a typical example. The user process makes a system call to send a character to the printer, and, as for any other ouput device, the first action is to place the character on a queue constructed from the buffer blocks of the dynamic buffering system. However, for the printer a count is kept of the number of characters waiting to be printed. If this is zero, a 'wake-up' signal is sent to the device-driver, and if the count exceeds a predetermined limit the system process 'sleeps' for a while before returning control to the user process. This ensures that the buffer pool is not swamped by printer ouput. The device-driver is woken up by the printer 'ready' interrupt, or by the signal from the user-level system call if the queue was previously empty, and it sends the next line of characters to be printed, then halts itself, to be reawoken by the next interrupt. If the printer has a single line buffer, this interrupt occurs when the line has been printed. If, however, the printer has a larger buffer, the interrupt will come before printing is complete, though this is transparent to the device-driver. However, if there is a large amount of material to be printed, the buffer will eventually fill up, and there must be some mechanism whereby the device-driver can be warned about this situation. A printer on a parallel interface can send a 'busy' signal which the driver can monitor by inspecting the status word. If the printer is on a serial interface, data flow control is usually achieved by use on 'X-ON/X-OFF Protocol'. This is exactly the same as the use of control-S and control-Q to stop and restart scrolling on a VDU. (X-ON and X-OFF are the names in the ASCII code for control-Q and control-S.) When the printer buffer is nearly full the printer sends an X-OFF code, and when the buffer has drained it sends an X-ON. The device-driver must treat the printer as both an output and an input device, reading the input line and watching for X-OFF and X-ON.

A printer is a non-shareable device, and in a multi-user system it is convenient to make it apparently shareable by using a *print spooler*. If a user wishes to print a file, he calls the print spooler which copies his file into a spool queue, sends a wake-up signal to the *printer daemon*, and returns control to the user. The printer daemon is a process which has exclusive use of the printer: it examines the spool queue, and if the queue is not empty, the daemon prints the next file, using the mechanisms already described. If the queue is empty, the daemon sleeps, and will be woken up by the arrival of the next file to print. The print spooler can also provide pagination facilities, adjustable margins, headings, etc., relieving individual programs of the need to look after these aspects of printing. (This use of the term 'spooler' should not be confused with the hardware 'print spoolers' that are marketed to speed up printing on single-user micros. These devices are just large RAM memories that can buffer the output for the printer, freeing the micro to get on with other tasks.)

7.6 SMART TERMINALS AND TRANSACTION PROCESSING

The multi-terminal handling system outlined in Sections 7.2 and 7.3 is appropriate to a multi-user system where each user is running his own program, quite independently of the other users. A rather different organization is required for a transaction processing system where a large number of terminals interact with a single program, e.g. an airline reservation system or a banking system. Such systems have three charac-teristics that influence the design of the communication subsystem. First, communication follows a strict protocol – the user makes a query, the system responds, the user replies . . . Second, because the terminals are operated by ticket clerks, bank tellers, etc., the dialogue is usually organ-ized on a form-filling basis – the system displays a form on the screen, with questions and spaces for answers (or lists of options). The clerk keys in responses, which must be validated before transmission to the computer. Third, since there are a large number of terminals, any one of which is only intermittently in use, it is uneconomic to provide a separ-

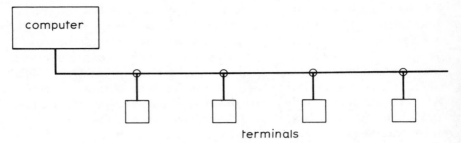

Fig. 7.1 'Multi-drop' terminal connection for transaction processing.

ate communication line for each – some sort of sharing is required. All three requirements are met by the use of 'smart' terminals with local processing power. When the system has transmitted a form to the screen, the filling in of the form by the operator is under control of the local processor in the terminal, and only when the reply is complete and validated is it transmitted. Thus the line is free for use by other terminals in the interim.

Because communication follows a strict protocol, it is possible to operate the terminals on a *polling* basis rather than an interrupt basis. The terminals are 'daisy chained' in the manner shown in Fig. 7.1, so that each terminal has lines only to its immediate neighbours. Effectively, all the terminals are connected by one line to the computer: this is sometimes called a 'multi-drop' connection. All messages in the system are prefixed by the address of the intended recipient, and the smart terminals only accept messages addressed to themselves. When a message is accepted it goes into the terminal's internal buffer, and hence to the screen. The software in the computer *polls* each terminal in turn, asking if the terminal has anything to transmit; the terminal can reply 'no' or 'yes'; in this latter case the acknowledgement is immediately followed by the transmitted data from the terminal buffer. The transmission is checked, and if an error is detected the computer requests retransmission, otherwise a positive acknowledgement is sent and the next terminal is polled. If the polling message elicits no reply after a certain time, the terminal is assumed to be unavailable, and the next terminal in sequence is polled.

When all the terminals have been polled, the communication software goes into 'output' mode. For each terminal in turn, if there is an output message waiting a polling message is sent asking 'ready to receive?' If a positive acknowledgement is sent back the message is transmitted: as before the transmission is checked, and retransmission is requested in the event of error. At the end of this output phase the communication software goes back to poll the terminals for incoming messages, and so the sequence continues.

Communication takes place a screenful at a time, and so the interface between the communication software and the transaction processing system consists of two screen buffers per terminal, one for an incoming message and one for an outgoing message. Associated with each buffer is a flag that is set to indicate that the buffer contents are valid. In this way the complexities of the communications subsystem are entirely hidden from the TP system.

7.7 COMMUNICATIONS PROCESSORS AND NETWORKS

Throughout this chapter we have assumed that the terminals are handled by the same processor that is running the rest of the operating system. This need not be so; terminal handling can be processor-intensive, and for reasons of efficiency it may be better to hive it off to a separate processor. The early mainframe computers were very poor at terminal handling, and it was quite common to use a minicomputer as a *'front end processor'* (FEP) to handle the communication lines. The FEP communicated with the main machine by means of a disc channel, so that it could read and write the memory of the main machine without using any of that machine's processor cycles. In a modern 'super-micro' there is often a dedicated 8-bit processor handling communications. This is attached to the system bus, and so can share memory with the main processor. The architecture we have outlined, in which there is a separate I/O buffer for each communication line forming a clean interface between I/O and the rest of the system, makes it easy to divide the operating system between two processors.

Connection of terminals by means of a front-end processor will relieve the load on the central machine. 'Local' terminals (i.e. situated in the same building as the computer, or in an adjacent building) can be connected by direct wires, but more distant terminals are connected by telephone lines (private circuits or 'dial-up' lines.) The simplest kind of communication network is the 'star' network (Fig. 7.2) in which each terminal has a direct connection to the computer (or front-end processor).

The economics of communicating over telephone lines may dictate variations in this simple scheme. If the terminals are clustered, it may be advantageous to use a *concentrator* to muliplex a number of terminals on to a single telephone line (Fig. 7.3). In the simplest case this is purely a hardware function: the terminals are multiplexed on to a single line, and demultiplexed at the computer end. Thus to the computer there is no difference between this and a simple star network. An alternative is to use a mini- or microcomputer as an *intelligent concentrator*. This handles terminal control, echoing, character translation and local editing (rub-out

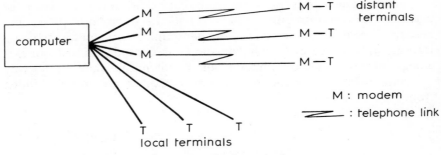

Fig. 7.2 Star network of terminals.

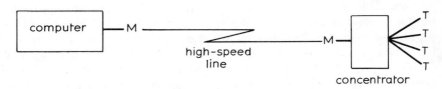

Fig. 7.3 Remote concentrator in a terminal network.

and line-delete). Thus the concentrator handles the device-level and physical-level I/O for the terminals connected to it, and communication with the main machine is in terms of complete print-lines. The communications software in the main machine performs *software demultiplexing* for input, and *software multiplexing* of output. Since it is dealing with complete lines of text, this is not a great burden.

It is common for the number of terminals available to users to exceed the number of physical connections (or *ports*) available on the machine. In this case the terminals are connected to a *port contention unit* which allocates ports on a first-come first-served basis, and informs terminals if there are no ports available. An extension of this idea is the PACX circuit switch, which allows a number of terminals to access ports on more than one machine. A user specifies the machine he wishes to use (and possibly the required line speed) by entering a suitable code from the keyboard. If a port is available an electrical connection is set up, and the PACX is thereafter transparent to the system. If intelligent concentrators are used, it is quite possible for them to have associated port contention units.

7.8 COMPUTER NETWORKS

A communications network provides *distribution of access*: the terminals are spread over a large geographical area. A true computer network provides *distribution of function*: the overall 'system' comprises a number of computer systems each providing certain functions that together make up the function of the whole. One example of distribution of function is found in the scientific research community. Here there is a requirement for a small number of 'super-computers' capable of doing very high speed floating-point operations, and a larger number of more conventional scientific machines. There may also be computers driving rather specialized experimental equipment. Another example is found in the commercial world. A large company operating on several sites may need a computer on each site to handle local affairs: these computers together comprise the corporate computer system, and when a corporate view is required they will have to communicate. A further example of distribution of function is specialization of software support. It may be sensible for certain packages to be run only at one site so that support for those packages does not need to be distributed throughout the organization. A final example comes from companies whose establishments are spread over different time-zones. In this case some establishments will be out of normal working hours while others are still working. The load on the overall system can therefore move around the computers, following the sun.

7.8.1   Network topology and message switching

It would not be economic for every computer in a network to be connected to every other computer. The pattern of connections is dictated by two requirements:

(1) Computers that generate a lot of communication between themselves usually have a direct connection.
(2) There must be at least one path between every pair of computers in the network, possibly involving an arbitrary number of other computers on the way.

The computers in a network are known as *hosts* (for irrelevant historical reasons). The host gains access to the network via a *network node* which is usually a small minicomputer. The benefit of this organization is that the host operating system is decoupled from the network. It sees the network as just another I/O channel, and so a minimum of software modification is required to interface to the network. Indeed, with this arrangement the network and the nodes can be operated as an autonomous 'transport service': this is how British Telecom's data transmission service PSS is operated.

The unit of communication between hosts is defined rather vaguely as a *message*. In general a message will pass through various nodes on its way to its destination, and the nodes must therefore operate on a store-and-forward basis.

A *wide-area-network* (WAN) therefore consists of a partially-connected mesh of nodes, with one or more hosts attached to each node. Messages flow through the network: if a node receives a message that is not destined for its host, it retransmits the message to the next node along the route.

7.8.2 Packet switching

The disadvantage of store-and-forward message transmission is that the node requires enough storage to handle a worst-case situation of several long messages arriving in parallel. The longer the messages, the more trouble this causes. However, we do not want to impose restrictions on message size, since we do not want the internal mechanisms of the network to impinge on the users. The problem is solved by breaking the message down into a sequence of short (typically 1k bits) *packets*. A store-and-forward node now needs only packet-sized storage, not message-sized storage. A transmitting node accepts a message from its host and disassembles it into packets; a receiving node reassembles the message and passes it to the host. Intermediate nodes simply retransmit packets as they arrive. In the simplest scheme each packet carries the full destination address as part of the *packet header*. A node examines the header to decide whether to retransmit or whether to assemble the packet into a message. If there is more than one route through the network between source and destination, there is no guarantee that all packets will follow the same route, and they may therefore arrive out of sequence. It is therefore necessary to include a sequence number in the header to facilitate reassembly of the message. An alternative organization is the *virtual call* mechanism used in British Telecom's PSS. A host wishing to transmit a message specifies the destination address. When the route has been established a *logical channel number* is assigned to be used in the packet headers. Tables are then set up in every node along the route to direct the packets, which follow each other in sequence as if there were a dedicated channel between the hosts.

7.8.3 Protocols

In order to communicate we need *protocols*, i.e. mutual agreement about message formats, control sequences, error signals, etc. The ultimate ideal is *open system interconnection* where we use the network like the telephone service: any computer or terminal can call up any other computer and exchange messages without prior arrangement. Although this is an ideal not attained in practice, we still want to be able to use the network without being concerned with all the details of its functioning. We thus want to establish a *host-to-host protocol* governing the exchange of information between process running in different hosts. We will also want a *file-transfer protocol* to allow transfer of files between computer systems.

In developing operating systems we have seen the benefits of building software in layers, each layer hiding a level of detail (e.g. processor-sharing) and providing an abstract-machine interface for the layers above. The same technique is used in network protocols: they are built up in layers, each layer hiding a level of detail from higher layers. The standard layered protocol is the ISO Reference Model, which is now briefly described.

(1) Level 1 is the physical transmission layer. This specifies electrical signals, connectors, etc. It provides physical transmission of a stream of bits from one site to another.
(2) Level 2 is the 'link' level. It provides a physical link with reliable (i.e. error-checked) transmission of blocks of bits called frames.
(3) Level 3 is the network level. It provides transfer of packets from one host to another, using a series of level 2 links.
(4) Level 4 is the transport level, providing process-to-process communication.
(5) Level 5 is the session level, providing management of resources (buffers, etc.).
(6) Level 6, called the 'presentation level', provides facilities such as file transfer.
(7) Level 7 is the application program level.

To get an idea of the interaction of these levels, consider the mechanisms of accessing a file held at a remote computer. An application program at level 7 issues an 'open file' call: the data-management section of the operating system recognizes that the file is held on a remote computer and invokes the file transfer protocol at level 6. The FTP process in the originating computer conducts a conversation with the FTP process in the remote computer using the level 4 host-to-host protocol. The processes appear to converse directly – the messages are in fact transmitted as packets by the lower level protocols. When the required file has been identified a level 5 protocol is invoked to effect physical transfer of the file. Again, the transfer actually involves all the lower level protocols.

7.8.4 Local area networks

A recent development is the local area network (LAN). As its name implies, it serves a local area – possibly as small as a single room, typically an area like a university campus or the premises of a particular business. Local area networks were developed to meet a need specific to microcomputers – the sharing of expensive resources. Microcomputers are cheap, but high-capacity disc stores, fast and/or good quality printers, etc. are expensive. The object of the LAN is to allow a number of microcomputers shared access to these expensive resources. Since the microcomputers are cheap, it is a necessary feature of a LAN that the method of connection to the network, and the network hardware itself, must also be cheap.

A local area network links a number of computers and a number of *servers* which provide communal facilities, e.g. file storage. (A server usually includes a small microprocessor for control purposes.) The computers and servers are known as *stations*. There are two methods of linking in common use, rings and broadcast networks.

In the ring method (often called a Cambridge Ring) all the stations are linked in a ring, which includes one special station, the *monitor station*, Information is transmitted in small (16-bit) packets, each packet including a source and destination address. The monitor station generates empty packets, which circulate round the ring. When a station wishes to transmit it waits for an empty packet to appear, then loads the addresses and data, marks the packet full, and sends it on its way. This process is repeated for each packet of the message. The *ring repeater* associated with each station examines packets as they go by to see if they are destined for that station. If not, they are retransmitted. If they are addressed to the station it may either accept or reject the packet. In either case control bits are set in the packet to indicate its fate. Eventually, the packet will reach its sender, who can see whether or not it was accepted, and by comparing the data content with a copy made before despatch it can verify that the transmission was correct. Within the stations, therefore, the operating system must be extended to provide packet assembly and disassembly. Apart from this, however, the ring appears as another peripheral. Protocols are needed to govern the transmission of data and requests for services.

In broadcast networks, all the stations are connected to a single linear cable (usually co-ax cable), and any transmission will be received by *all* stations. Fortunately it is simple for the hardware to recognize when a transmission is in progress ('carrier sense') and a station therefore waits for the line to be free before transmitting. However, because of the propagation delays along the cable it is possible for two stations to recognize the line as free and start transmitting simultaneously. This causes a clash, which garbles the messages. Again, fortunately, the hardware can sense this clash, and if it is discovered the station backs off and waits a *random* time before retransmitting. In this way the problems of sharing a line are overcome. Once connection is established the message is transmitted in packets of up to 4k bits.

The broadcast network is often called 'Ethernet', because that was the first system to use the technique. The relative merits of the Ethernet versus the Cambridge Ring are hotly debated. A substantial advantage of broadcast techniques is that the ring connection is trivial, whereas ring systems need a repeater at each station. The repeaters require power, which they draw from the ring. Another benefit of the broadcast systems is that they are not affected by failure of a station, whereas failure of a ring repeater incapacitates the whole ring.

Whichever technology is used, local area networks are a development of the greatest importance. In the same way as programming is simplified by an approach that thinks in terms of small procedures/programs, each doing a well-defined job, the computer system of tomorrow is likely to be made up of lots of small systems, each doing a specific job, linked by a local area network.

8

The user interface

8.1 COMPONENTS OF THE USER INTERFACE

Now at last we come to the user interface. In discussing and designing operating systems, it is easy to lose sight of the fact that the only reason for all the infrastructure is in fact to provide the facilities for the user to do what he wants to do. We now consider the kinds of thing that a user will require from the operating system, and the ways in which these things can be provided.

The most obvious user interface is the command language interpreter, which takes commands from the keyboard and causes them to be obeyed, and it is easy to think that this (or its equivalent in a batch environment) constitutes the whole of the user interface. In fact, there is a much more fundamental interface provided by the *system calls*. These are the entries to the kernel which allow programs to manipulate files, devices and processes. Some authors would go so far as to claim that the system calls define the whole of the user interface, but we shall not take so extreme a view. The command language interpreter (or its batch equivalent) uses the system calls to cause the operating system to perform the actions required by the user. In a sense we can say that the system calls define an abstract machine that has the facilities required to implement an interactive (batch) environment, and for that reason they are sometimes described as constituting the 'software instruction set'.

8.2 SYSTEM CALLS

Before looking at the detail of system calls, it is worth noting that there is an important distinction between systems that allow open access to the system calls, and those that restrict access. At one extreme, 'normal' programs can be denied any direct access to the system calls; systems of this kind usually allow a program to generate a text stream that will be interpreted as if it had been typed in at the keyboard. (The 'virtual terminals' of DEC's RSTS-E system are a typical example of this approach.) At the other extreme, systems like UNIX allow free access to the system calls; subject only to having the necessary permissions to read/execute the files involved, programs can do anything that could be achieved from the keyboard (and a few more things besides!) In the middle are systems (typically mainframe systems like ICL's VME) that restrict system call access to simple file and I/O device manipulations, on the doubtful principle that 'the system knows best'. The important consequence of limiting access to system calls is that the limitation makes the command language interpreter an indissoluble part of the operating system, whereas open access to system calls makes the command language interpreter just another program. Thus on restrictive systems the command language interpreter tends to be 'feature oriented', since the designer tries (usually unsuccessfully) to anticipate everything a user might want to do. Open access to system calls makes it possible to offer several command language interpreters, since there is nothing very special about them. Thus a simple 'menu' interface can be provided for naïve users, while the specialists have access to a very powerful command language.

8.2.1   System calls in CP/M

The system calls of CP/M are provided in a hardware-independent manner by BDOS. The convention is that in all CP/M systems, a JMP instruction to the BDOS entry point is stored at address 0005H, so that system call addresses will not depend on the actual memory allocation. To call a system function the user places the 'system call number' in the C register, and possibly loads other registers with parameters for the system call – each system call defines its own requirements. The program then executes a CALL to 0005H to perform the system function. (It is common to use the assembler to define a symbol BDOS with the value 0005H, so that in a program the system facilities are accessed by 'CALL BDOS'.) A selection of the CP/M system calls is given in Table 8.1. As would be expected for a single-user system, they are restricted to input–output and file-system manipulation. These system calls provide the machine-independent interface for the great mass of CP/M software on the market.

8.2.2   System calls in UNIX

In UNIX, system calls can be made either from programs written in C or (very rarely) from assembler programs. The system calls appear to the C programmer as a set of predefined functions, so they are very easy to use. Ease of use is increased even more by the provision of a number of files containing type declarations for the structures used as parameters to the system calls. A standard C facility allows these files to be easily incorporated in a program, so that the program line

include <stdio.h>

is all that is needed to enable the input–output system calls to be used without any additional declarations. The system calls also follow standard conventions regarding error reporting: each system call returns a value to indicate whether the requested operation has been successfully performed (zero) or has failed (minus one). In the case of failure the cause

Table 8.1   A selection of CP/M system calls

0	Warm boot. Reads command interpreter and BIOS from disc.
1	Console input. Reads character from console.
2	Console output. Sends character to console.
3	Reader input. Reads character from reader device.
4	Punch output. Sends character to 'punch' device.
5	List output. Sends character to 'list' device (usually printer).
6	Direct console I/O. Read/write console 'raw', i.e. no processing of characters.
7	Get IOBYTE. Determine current allocation of devices.
8	Set IOBYTE. Change allocation of devices.
9	Print string. Print string of characters from memory buffer.
10	Read console buffer. Read line of input, with in-line editing.
11	Get console status. Test whether there is a character waiting from the console.
12	Return version number. Returns version number of this version of CP/M.
13	Reset disc system.
14	Select disc. Select disc A or B for subsequent operations.
15	Open file. Open a file that already exists.
16	Close file. Close a file that already exists.
17	Search for file. Determine if the named file exists on disc.
18	Search for file. If call 17 has found a file matching a 'wild-card' name, determine if there is another file that also matches the specification.
19	Delete file. Delete named file and make space available for reuse.
20	Read sequential. Read next record from open file.
21	Write sequential. Write next record to open file.
22	Create file.
23	Rename file.
28	Write to protected disc.
30	Set file attributes.
33	Read record, random access.
34	Write record, random access.

is indicated by setting an error number in a pre-declared global variable, 'errno'. The main system calls of UNIX are listed in Table 8.2; they have been classified under several broad headings since they cover a wider range of functions than just input–output and file manipulation. As with CP/M, these system calls define the machine-independent interface which makes UNIX software transportable.

Table 8.2 Some UNIX system calls

Input–output
>open(name, mode)
>>open file or device in specified mode. Returns a file descriptor for subsequent use.

>close(fd)
>>close file specified by descriptor fd.

>read(fd, buffer, nbytes)
>>read up to nbytes into buffer from file described by fd.

>write(fd, buffer, nbytes)
>>write nbytes from buffer to file described by fd.

>pipe(fd2)
>>set up an interprocess communication channel, placing file descriptors to be used for reading and writing in the 2-element array fd2.

>ioctl(fd, request, argptr)
>>test and set properties of terminals, etc.

File system management
>access(name, mode)
>>determine if file 'name' can be accessed in specified mode.

>chdir(dirname)
>>select new working directory.

>chmod(name, mode)
>>change permissions for file 'name' as specified by 'mode'.

>chown(name, owner, group)
>>allows system manager (only!) to change file ownership.

>creat(name, mode)
>>create new file with specified mode.

>link(name1, name2)
>>establish 'name2' as an alias for file 'name1'

>mount(dummy, name, rwflag)
>>mount the file system 'name' on the directory 'dummy'.

>umount(name)
>>unmount a file system previously mounted.

>stat(name, buffer)
>>record status of file 'name' in buffer.

>unlink(name)
>>remove the file 'name' from its directory.

Process management

fork()

spawn new process.

wait(status)

wait until child process terminates, and record termination status.

alarm(seconds)

send a signal to the process after 'seconds' delay.

execl(name, arg0, arg1,. . ., argn, 0)

ovelay code of current process image from file 'name' and make arg0 . . . argn available as arguments to new code.

exit(status)

terminate process and report 'status' to parent.

kill(pid, sig)

send signal 'sig' to process number 'pid'

nice(priority)

decrease priority of a process that is to run in the background.

pause()

wait for signal from kill or alarm.

signal

used to specify action to be taken when a signal is received – ignore, default action or call named function.

Other system calls

getpid

Return process ID of current process. (Useful for generating unique names for files.)

getuid

returns user identity.

setuid

allows the super-user to change user identification.

8.3   THE INTERACTIVE INTERFACE

The interactive interface is provided by a *command language interpreter* (CLI) which reads command lines from the keyboard and carries out the specified actions. A command consists of a *command name*, possibly followed by one or more *arguments*. Some simple commands are obeyed directly by the CLI, but most commands require loading of a program from disc. In this case the command program must transfer control back to the CLI on termination (normal or abnormal).

8.3.1   **Implementing the interactive interface**

In CP/M, the CLI is loaded into memory, at the top of the Transient Program Area, just bleow the BDOS. Its action can be summarized as follows.

issue a prompt
read a line from the console device
extract command word
if command word is DIR, ERA, REN, TYPE or SAVE then obey the
command and go back to issue a prompt
else
>   set up file descriptor(s) for the file(s) given as arguments (if any)
>   look for a file with the same name as the command word and
>   extension '.COM'.
>   if such a file exists, load it into the TPA and transfer control to it,
>   otherwise send an error message to the screen and start over.

All CP/M command programs must transfer control back to the CLI on termination. A command that requires a large amount of memory is allowed to overwrite the CLI; on termination it must transfer control to the 'warm boot' entry in BDOS, which will reload the CLI from the disc. Note that the CLI will use the CP/M system calls to communicate with the keyboard and to load files from disc. In particular, reading of the command line will be achieved by a call on 'read console buffer', so that the CLI will wait at this point until a complete line has been typed. Using the system call means also that the user can use the in-line editing facilities of CP/M while typing in his commands.

In a multi-user system there will be a separate process for each user, each such process running a separate copy of the CLI. Thus the simplest multi-user system (for example, MP/M) merely sets up a process for each user with a command language interpreter that operates exactly in the way described above. The setting up of the processes for each user will usually involve some authentication by means of user identifiers and passwords.

However, in a system based on a process architecture it is possible to provide the user with more facilities quite simply. For example, in a CP/M-type system only one command can be obeyed at once: if a slow compilation is started, the CLI will not be able to accept another command until the compilation finishes. The alternative is for the CLI to create a new process for each command. If the CLI chooses to wait for the child process to finish, it will behave like a CP/M system, but it is possible for the user to request that the command process run in parallel with the CLI, thus giving the possibility of 'foreground–background' working. This is the technique adopted in UNIX, and we now give a brief account of the way in which UNIX implements the interactive interface.

When a UNIX system is first started, one 'primeval' process called init is initiated. The first action of init is to create a process for each terminal that is known to the system; this will be referred to as the 'terminal process'. At first, the terminal process runs a program called 'getty' which sets up the hardware interface to suit the characteristics (speed, parity, etc.) of the terminal (as recorded in a file), issues a 'login' message, and waits for terminal input. When a user types in his identifier, getty is replaced by the login program, which prompts the user for his password. If the user is satisfactorily authenticated, the login program overwrites itself with the 'shell' program, which is the UNIX command language interpreter, and which now takes over control of the terminal. When the user eventually logs out, the terminal process kills itself. The init process has meanwhile been sleeping, having requested a signal whenever one of its offspring processes dies. The logout will thus activate init, which creates a new terminal process running getty, and the whole cycle is repeated.

As already mentioned, when a command is obeyed, the shell creates a new process to run the command. Normally, the shell will then just wait for the command process to terminate, but it is possible for the shell to continue running in parallel with the command process, thus giving 'foreground–background' working. Thus it is possible to initiate a long compilation and to leave it running in the background while editing or performing other terminal activity.

8.3.2 User authentication

In a multi-user system some sort of protection is required to ensure that a user cannot gain illicit access to another user's files, and the first component of the interactive interface is the authentication of a user who tries to access the system. This is usually done by requesting a password: only if the user can give the password known to the system is he allowed access. To be effective, there are two requirements of a password protection system. First, it must be easy for a user to change his password – systems where passwords can only be changed by the system administrator are inflexible. Second, it is imperative that nowhere in the system should there be a file containing the passwords in their original form. If such a file exists (as it does on many older systems), it is only a matter of time before a malevolent user succeeds in accessing it, and the security of the system is lost. Instead, passwords should be encrypted, with only the encryption recorded in the system. Use of a 'trap-door' encryption method (i.e. one for which the inverse transformation is impossible) then ensures a reasonable degree of security for passwords. Needless to say, terminal echo should be turned off whenever a password is to be typed in.

8.3.3 **The command language environment**

The command language defines the environment in which interactive use of the system takes place. Early systems had a fixed repertoire of commands, built into the command language interpreter. A general escape mechanism was provided by a 'RUN' command which caused a program in a named file to be run. In this way subsystems could be accessed, essentially extending the environment provided by the command language. More modern systems use the technique (already noted in connection with CP/M) of taking the command name as the name of an executable file, and finding that file on the disc. This gives a completely general and extensible facility. UNIX takes this approach further: the command name is taken as a file name, and that file is sought first in the user's directory, then in a predefined sequence of system directories; in this way users can redefine commands if they wish, since their version will be found first. Alternatively, a full path name can be given instead of a command name: this will cause the named file to be executed.

Commands consist of a command name, possibly followed by arguments. It is very desirable that different commands should have a uniform format, and follow uniform conventions about arguments. Indeed, one of the major disadvantages of the 'subsystem' approach is that each subsystem tends to have its own conventions, quite different from those of any other subsystem. Most commands take either no arguments or one filename as argument, and so there is some merit in the CP/M approach which allows zero, one or two arguments for a command. The CLI assumes that if arguments are present they are file names, and sets up file descriptors before loading the executable file. As usual, UNIX provides more elaborate facilities in a well-thought-out way. Commands can have any number of arguments: the shell parses the command line to identify the arguments, and makes them available as text strings to the command when it starts execution. Thus the interpretation of an argument as a file name or otherwise is up to the command. Most commands follow a set of uniform conventions for arguments, e.g. options precede file-name arguments, and are introduced by a minus sign. The UNIX shell also sets up the 'standard input' and 'standard ouput' channels before starting execution of a command. These are normally the keyboard and screen respectively, but shell syntax allows the command line to specify redirection of either or both to/from files. Thus a program written to send output to a VDU can be made to send its output to a file by changing the command line that calls the program rather than changing the program itself. The usefulness of this feature is enhanced even more by the fact that in UNIX there is a uniformity between files and devices: all devices appear in a directory as if they were files, and a graph-plotter might be accessed, for example, as the 'file' '/dev/gp'.

A further useful component of the command language environment is the ability to obey a sequence of commands from a file as if they had been typed at the keyboard. (Such a file is often called an 'indirect command file' or, sometimes, confusingly, a 'batch' file.) The simplest way to provide this facility is to include a 'run' command whose argument is the name of the file containing the command sequence. An elegant feature of UNIX is that if a command name matches the name of a file marked 'executable' but containing text, it is assumed to be an indirect command file and the commands therein are obeyed.

8.4   THE BATCH INTERFACE

Batch working is nowadays restricted to commercial data processing installations and large scientific 'number-crunching' systems; in both cases it is done on large mainframe computers that operate under the control of elaborate and complex operating systems (e.g. IBM's MVS). These systems have evolved over many years, and do not in general have the sort of structure that is typical of the systems described in this book. However, it is of interest to see how a batch system could be implemented in a process-based environment, and to consider some of the special problems that batch operation poses for the designer of an operating system.

8.4.1   Implementing the batch interface

It is in fact very easy to implement a batch system in a process-based architecture. We saw in Chapter 2 how a spooling system could be constructed using three programs (reader, writer and job supervisor) running in a pseudo-concurrent manner under the control of a multi-programming executive. In a process-based operating system the reader, writer and job supervisor become processes, and are then run concurrently along with the other processes of the system by the kernel. In practice, it would probably be better to create a single process for each batch stream: this process would then create the reader, writer and job supervisor as 'child' processes. The interaction of these processes is exactly as described in Chapter 2, and it is a trivial matter to implement the more complicated spooling systems described in that chapter by setting up processes to correspond to the programs making up the system in the older framework.

8.4.2   **Facilities of the batch interface**

The facilities of the batch interface are essentially those of the spooling systems already described. At the simplest, the user submits a job on a deck of cards, and these jobs are batched together to run in sequence. However, in a modern environment it is likely that the job will be more complex than the simple 'program + data' of the early systems, e.g. a data processing program is likely to access a master file, a transactions file and an updated master file. Also, the program itself is likely to be held in a file rather than on cards. Finally, the job will probably involve more than the simple 'compile and run' of the spooling systems already described; it is likely to be made up of a number of job steps, some of which may be conditional on the successful completion of earlier job steps. Thus a batch job is usually presented to the operating system as a *job description* written in a specialized *job control language*. This job description describes the job steps and their sequencing, details the files to be used by each step, and defines the connections to be made between these files and the input–output 'channels' seen by the programs that comprise the job. The job description may also include scheduling information (e.g. priority) and may also specify limits on the use of resorces such as CPU time. The job description may be submitted on cards, or may be entered from a terminal, in which case the mode of working is described as *conversational remote job entry*. The form of the job control language is described in Section 8.5.

In a data-processing environment the jobs run in a batch system are all very similar in requirements (e.g. mainly file updating or report generation). In a scientific computing environment (e.g. one serving a large laboratory) the jobs are likely to be of a much more varied character, and to come from a much larger user population. In such an environment the batch system may incorporate a measure of control so as to allocate computing facilities fairly amongst a large number of competing users. Typically this is done by an *accounting subsystem* which records for each job items such as

Processor time used
Elapsed time
Memory usage
Peripheral activity

These quantities can be printed out at the end of a job, and can also be used to compute a notional 'charge' for the job, which can be debited against the user's budget. The system can reject jobs from users who have used up their budget for the current accounting period, and the charging information can be used to assess priorities, e.g. decreasing priority for a user who has been using his budget at a rate in excess of some norm. Many sophisticated variants of this kind of scheme have been incorporated into systems serving universities, but this kind of control is less common in industrial environments.

8.4.3 Resource allocation in batch systems

A problem that arises in batch systems, though not in interactive systems, is the allocation of non-shareable resources. In an interactive environment the user can be told if the resource he wants is not available, and can decide for himself what action to take. In a batch system the user is by definition not available to intervene in the running of the job, and so the operating system must administer the resources. The simplest strategy is to allocate *all* the resources needed by a job before the job starts; in this way the system can ensure that the job will be able to run to completion. However, this strategy may lead to scarce resources being idle for long periods. For example, suppose that the installation has one high-quality plotter. A job may perform a very long computation preparing the information to be plotted, and does not actually need the plotter until the computation is finished. If the plotter is allocated to the job right from the start it will be idle, yet unavailable to other users, while the computation is in progress. It is therefore desirable to adopt a dynamic allocation strategy in which programs request resources when they actually require them, so as to increase the utilization of resources in a multi-programming environment. To revert to our previous example, the program will request the graph plotter only when it has finished the computation, so that until that time the plotter is available for use by other programs. If the plotter is not free at the time it is required the program will have to wait until it becomes free. This is not a great handicap in a multi-programming system, since there will be other jobs for the processor to get on with. The operating system must associate a queue of requests for allocation of a non-shareable device so that the competing programs get the device in order of request time, or in accordance with some priority ranking, as determined by the system administrator.

If programs have access to several non-shareable resources there is a danger of *deadlock* occurring. For example, suppose that two programs P1 and P2 require resources R1 and R2, and suppose that the sequence is as follows:

P1: . . . . . . request R1 . . . request R2 . . . release R1 . . . release R2

P2: . . . . . . request R2 . . . request R1 . . . release R2 . . . release R1

If the two programs are multi-programmed together, there is a possibility of deadlock if P1 requests R2 before P2 has released it, and P2's request for R1 is made before P1 has released it. If this occurs both processes will be halted, each waiting for the other to do something, and deadlock ensues.

The problem of deadlock prevention (or avoidance) has received a lot of attention from computer scientists, and many elaborate algorithms have been proposed. However, most systems in practice do not incorporate these algorithms: they include some common-sense precautions which reduce the chance of deadlock, and accept the possibility that deadlock may sometimes occur. For example, in IBM's OS/370 jobs are divided up into a sequence of *job steps*, e.g. compile, link-edit, run. Files are allocated to a job at the start, but all other resources have to be relinquished at the end of a job step, and rerequested if they are needed for the next job step. Thus although a resource may be idle for part of a job step, at the end of the job step it comes 'up for grabs', and competing jobs get a chance to acquire the resource. At the start of a job step resources are acquired in the order files first, then memory, then peripherals, so as to avoid deadlock between multiple copies of the job-step initiator. If a deadlock does occur, it is left to the human operator to detect and then resolve it. The detection consists of the operator noticing a lack of activity in the system – experienced operators can spot a deadlock almost as soon as it occurs. Resolution of the deadlock is achieved by aborting jobs until the log-jam clears, then rerunning the aborted jobs. If a job updates a master file it may not be safe to rerun it. The job control language allows the user to specify 'no rerun', and such a job will normally be written with restart points built in, so that if it gets aborted it can be restarted in a safe manner.

In a sophisticated spooling system the resource allocation will interact with the high-level scheduling. It will be recalled that the high-level scheduler selects the mix of jobs to be multi-programmed. Obviously, there is no point in including in the mix two jobs which are competing for the same resource, nor should the total requirement for a resource (e.g. magnetic tape drives) over the jobs in the mix exceed the total physical resource available. In practice the most commonly used batch systems are not highly sophisticated, and the selection of the job mix is mainly at the discretion of an experienced operator.

8.5   COMMAND LANGUAGES

The command language is the primary interface between the system and the user, and the facilities it provides determine the user's perception of the system as a help or a hindrance. Much could be written about the design of command languages, but in this section we merely give a few examples of typical languages and their facilities to give the reader some impression of how different systems approach the problem. Historically, interactive command languages and batch command languages have developed along different routes, and we shall describe them separately. Finally we shall discuss briefly the development of integrated operating system command languages (OSCLs) and the attempts to develop international standards in this field.

8.5.1   Interactive command languages

For interactive work the command language requirement appears at first sight to be trivial. Commands consist of a command name (or verb) possibly followed by arguments, and are obeyed one at a time as they are typed in by the user. The major differences between systems are in the range of commands available, and in the way the system addresses the user. Some systems (e.g. CP/M, UNIX) are terse, with very short command names and minimal responses, while others have long 'meaningful' command names (e.g. 'deletefilesofuser') and engage the user in a verbose dialogue. In modern systems there is a trend towards screen menus as a user-friendly interface.

Even at the level of simple interactive commands, though, useful refinements can be built in. Most systems allow a 'wild card' facility in naming files, usually accepting asterisk as a match for an arbitrary string of characters in a file name, and query as a match for a single character, so that '*.BAS' will match all file names that end in '.BAS', and 'PROG?.BAS' will match 'PROG1. BAS', 'PROG2. BAS', etc. In CP/M this facility is built into the disc-handling software: in UNIX the same facility is provided in a rather different way. When parsing a command line the UNIX shell expands any 'wild card' names into a list of all matching file names, sorted in alphabetical order, and makes the names available as arguments to the command, just as if they had been typed by the user. Thus *all* commands, including user-written commands, can make use of the wild card facility, rather than it being restricted only to the built-in commands. This is an example of the UNIX philosophy of making facilities that are likely to be of general use available on a system-wide basis so that the same facility does not have to be coded into lots of different commands. Another powerful facility provided by the UNIX shell is *input–output redirection*. Many commands are written to take input (if required) from the keyboard and send output to the screen. Shell syntax allows the user to specify that input is to come from a file, or output is to go to a file. Thus the command ls

displays a list of the files in user's directory on the screen:

ls > catalog

sends the list to the file 'catalog' instead. Similarly,

ed foobar

calls the editor to edit the file 'foobar', taking editing commands from the keyboard, while

ed foobar < script

will edit foobar, but will read the editing commands from the file 'script'. Again, this is a shell facility and so is available to all commands; it is not necessary to build a file-output option into every command.

The concept of input–output redirection is extended in UNIX to the enormously useful *pipe*. A pipe is a connection between two commands or programs so that the output of the first becomes the input of the second. Pipes make it easy to string together lots of simple programs to produce a complicated program. Thus suppose 'prog1' is the name of a file containing an executable program that displays a sequence of names on the screen on consecutive lines, and suppose it is required to display the names in alphabetical order. The user could of course change his program to do the sorting, but it is much easier to use the UNIX utility 'sort', which by default reads the standard input channel, sorts into alphabetical order and outputs the lines in sorted order on the standard output channel (normally connected to the screen). A program can be executed by just giving its file name as a command, so

prog1

would cause the program to run, sending unsorted output to the screen. The command

prog1 | sort

will run prog1 and 'pipe' its output into the next command, sort. This will do the sorting and output the sorted list to the screen. Pipes are a major component in the UNIX 'building brick' philosophy of programming; it is interesting to note that the concepts of pipes and input–output redirection, exploited for many years in UNIX, are at last beginning to appear in other operating systems (e.g. MS-DOS 2).

A further useful facility provided by the shell is *command substitution*, which allows the output of one command to be treated as the arguments of another command. To see the use of this, consider the electronic mail facility of UNIX. The sequence.

>   mail liona nicola julia
>   Hi there!
>   control-D

will put the message 'Hi there!' into the mail-boxes of the named users so that when they next log in they will receive the message. (Control-D is the end-of-file character.) Now suppose we want to send messages to various groups of users. If a file 'mail__list' contains the user-identifiers of the intended recipients.

>   mail `cat mail__list` < message

will do the trick. 'cat mail__list' would normally display the contents of file mail__list on the screen: enclosing it in grave accents within the mail command ensures that the output that would normally go to the screen is instead presented as a sequence of arguments to the mail command. The input diversion '< message' indicates that the input to mail is to come from the file 'message' rather than from the keyboard. Thus we see how different features of the shell can be combined to give a remarkably powerful interactive language.

Most interactive systems allow 'command files', where a sequence of commands is taken from a file instead of from the keyboard. This is a useful shorthand for commonly occurring operations that require a number of commands. In UNIX the idea is taken further. We have already seen that the name of an executable file containing text can be used as a command, and causes the text contained in the file to be presented to the shell as if it had come from the terminal. It is thus very easy to define new commands in this way, and immediately there comes the need to be able to pass arguments to a command file. This is allowed by the shell. Suppose that 'com' is the name of an executable text file containing shell commands, and the user types

>   com   arg__1   arg__2   arg__3

Then while the commands in the file are being executed, the arguments arg__1, arg__2 and arg__3 can be assessed as $1, $2 and $3 respectively. (There is a close parallel here with macros in assembly language programming.) Alternatively, $* stands for the complete argument string.

As an illustration, consider the following problem. The C compiler in UNIX always leaves the compiled program in a file called 'a.out'. A user wishes to define a command that will compile the source program and immediately execute the compiled version. He sets up a file called crun which contains the following:

```
cc $1
a.out
```

and makes the file executable. Now the command

```
crun thing.c
```

will execute the command 'cc thing.c', followed by the command 'a.out' which causes the compiled program to be executed. However, this is restrictive: the source program must be in a single file, and no options can be specified for the call of the C compiler. It would be better to use

```
cc $*
a.out
```

so that whatever argument string is given for the crun command is passed intact to the cc command.

This little example can be used to demonstrate the need for more elaborate 'programming' facilities in a command language. Consider what happens if the C compiler finds errors in the program. Suitably cryptic messages will be sent to the terminal, but the crun command will still try to execute the file a.out, even though the compiler has not created it. What is likely to happen is that there will be an a.out file from a previous compilation, and that will get executed. What is required is something like

```
if there is an a.out file, remove it
call the C compiler
if there is now an a.out file, execute it
```

Fortunately, UNIX provides quite powerful 'programming' facilities that make this kind of thing possible. It has an 'if . . . then . . . else' construct, and a primitive for testing file status. The contents of the crun file would be as follows:

```
if test -f a.out
then rm a.out
```

```
fi
cc $*
if test -f a.out
then a.out
fi
```

Another common requirement in shell command files is to loop, applying the same operations to each file presented as an argument. For example, suppose we want to define a command to remove all blank lines from one or more files. The skeleton of such a command file is

```
for i in $*
ed – $i < script
done
```

The 'for' statement causes the editor to be called to edit each argument in turn, so that any number of arguments can be given to the command. 'script' is a file containing the editing commands to remove blank lines. In practice, one prefers to incorporate the editing commands in the command file, using a shell capability to specify that standard input is to be diverted to come from the command file. The final version of our command is

```
for i in $*
  ed – << !
    g/^$/d
    w
!
done
```

The notation << ! indicates that what follows, up to the matching ! is to be taken as standard input, and so will be read by the editor instead of keyboard input. The string g/^$/d is the editor command to delete all blank lines(!) and the w causes the file to be written back to disc in its changed form.

We have only touched on the surface of the extensive programming capability of the UNIX shell. It provides while loops, case statements, variables, expressions – almost everything you expect in a high-level language (though with an unpalatable syntax). Regrettably, there is not space to pursue the subject in more detail here.

8.5.2 Batch command languages

Batch command languages are generally known as *job control languages* and referred to by the acronym, JCL. The best known (and most universally detested) JCL is that used on the IBM mainframes, and an example of its use is given here to demonstrate the flavour of mainframe computing.

Figure 8.1 shows (approximately) the JCL required to run a FORTRAN compile-and-run job on a typical IBM installation. The appearance will be familiar to anyone who has used a mainframe assembler, since the format is exactly that of an assembler – each line contains an optional label, an operation and some arguments. The arguments are, as in many assemblers, couched in a syntax that consists almost entirely of brackets, commas and equals signs. The origin of JCL in the punched card era is also apparent: each statement starts with two strokes in columns one and two to identify it as a JCL statement, and if a statement extends over more than one line a continuation marker is required in the rightmost column of the first line.

```
 1.   //C         EXEC    PGM=IEYFORT,PARM='SOURCE'
 2.   //SYSPRINT   DD      SYSOUT=A
 3.   //SYSLIN     DD      DSNAME=SYSL.UT4,DISP=OLD              X
 4.   //                   DCB=(RECFM=FB,LRECL=80.BLKSIZE=800)
 5.   //G         EXEC    PGM=FORTLINK,COND=(4,LT,C)
 6.   //SYSPRINT   DD      SYSOUT=A
 7.   //SYSLIN     DD      DSNAME=*.C.SYSLIN,DISP=OLD
 8.   //SYSLIB     DD      DSNAME=SYSL.FORTLIB,DISP=OLD
 9.   //FT03F001   DD      DDNAME=SYSIN
10.   //FT05F001   DD      DDNAME=SYSIN
11.   //FT06F001   DD      DDNAME=PRINT
12.   //FT07F001   DD      UNIT=SYSCP
13.   //PRINT      DD      SYSOUT=A,DCB=(RECFM=FA,BLKSIZE=133)
```

Fig. 8.1 Example of JCL for IBM mainframe (note that the line numbers are present for the purposes of explanation, and are not part of the JCL, which starts with the two solidi in 'card columns' 1 and 2).

The job consists of two steps: the first step is the FORTRAN compilation, and the second step links in the precompiled library subroutines and executes the resulting program. This second step must only be executed if no errors were reported by the compiler. For each step the JCL must set up the environment in which the program runs, specifying the files ('datasets' in IBM terminology) to be used, and their relation to the filenames used in the programs. For communication between job-steps it is necessary to be able to relate files used by one job-step to those created by an earlier job-step.

The general form of the job control for a job step is an 'EXEC' command to execute a program, followed by a number of data definition (DD) commands that specify the datasets to be used by that program. Thus line 1 of the example calls for the execution of the FORTRAN compiler (IEYFORT), and lines 2,3 and 4 define the datasets to be used by the compiler. In the 'label' field immediately after the slashes is the name of the dataset, and the 'operand' field defines (entirely or in part) the properties of the dataset. The operating system associates a 'data control block' with each dataset, which completely defines the dataset. The contents of this DCB can be set up at the time the dataset was created, by the JCL, or at run-time by the program. The JCL can override settings already in the DCB, as can the run-time program; this gives a convenient mechanism for establishing default values for various parameters.

The FORTRAN compiler used in this example always takes its input from punched cards on the same device as the JCL, so only its output datasets need to be defined. There are two of these, SYSPRINT for the listing and error messages, and SYSLIN to hold the compiled program. SYSPRINT is to be sent to a spooled printer, so the data definition is given as 'SYSOUT=A' which defines a specific printer or class of printers. The output from the compiler is to be placed on a specific disc-drive; however, to allow for hardware reconfigurations programmers do not refer to devices by absolute name. Instead the system maintains a list that maps logical names on to actual devices. Thus the dataset SYSLIN is to be placed on device with dataset (DSNAME) 'SYSL.UT4' ('unit 4 on the SYStem List'). 'DISP=OLD' specifies that this is not a new dataset to be created, and finally the format of the dataset is declared by the DCB argument to be 'fixed block size, blocked records, logical record length 80, blocksize 800'. Note the continuation marker in this JCL statement. Note also that, before leaving the compiler the EXEC statement has been given a label so that it can be referred to later. The argument 'PARM='SOURCE' ' is a crude mechanism provided within JCL for passing options to programs. The option is passed to the program as a string, and the program can do what it likes with it. In this case, it specifies that the compiler should produce a source listing.

The remainder of the JCL (lines 5 to 13) defines the load-and-go sequence. Line 5, labelled G, EXEC's a program called FORTLINK that will link-edit and run the compiled FORTRAN program. It specifies that this should only happen if there were no errors detected, but in the most contorted way. All programs on termination leave a 'condition code' in a specific register, and this can be tested by the COND parameter in the JCL. The sequence 'COND=(4,LT,C)' says 'omit this step if 4 is less than the condition code returned by the preceding step'. Lines 6 to 8 define the files used in the link-editing stage; line 6 defines a SYSPRINT for diagnostic information, and lines 7 and 8 define the input datasets – SYSLIN the main input, and SYSLIB the library of precompiled subroutines. SYSLIN must of course be the same dataset as was used by the compiler, and on line 7 we see an example of a backward reference on a data definition. The expression '*.C.SYSLIN' denotes a backward reference to step C, and in particular the dataset SYSLIN defined therein. The library is part of the system library, and in line 8 is defined as SYSL.FORTLIB. The remaining lines define the datasets to be used at run time. FORTRAN describes input–output in terms of numbered channels, and there is a convention within the operating system that channel n corresponds to a dataset named 'FT0nF001'. Lines 9 and 11 show how commonly occurring data-descriptions can be specified only once; 'DDNAME=PRINT' indicates that the definition of this dataset will be found in the line labelled PRINT, so that FT03F001 and FT06F001 both refer to a spooled printer (SYSOUT=A) with fixed records of which the first byte is a printer control character (RECFM=FA), and a block size of 133 bytes. On line 10 there is another use of DDNAME, this time referring to a system-defined dataset, the system card reader; this is assigned to channel 5. Finally channel 7 is to be the system card punch: UNIT indicates a request for a specific device, and SYSCP defines the device to be a system card punch.

All this to compile and run a simple FORTRAN program! In practice things are not so bad: the JCL given in Fig. 8.1 is filed away as a macro (IBM use the term 'catalog procedure') with the name FORTRAN, say, and the user would merely have to write

```
//      EXEC   FORTRAN
```

to invoke it. Indeed, instead of tying input to the system card reader, the compiler would be written to read from dataset SYSLIN, and for simple card input the calling sequence would be

```
//              EXEC   FORTRAN
//C. SYSIN   DD   *
<cards>
/*
```

In the DD statement, 'C.SYSIN' indicates that this is a definition of SYSLIN for step C, and the asterisk indicates that the dataset follows on cards, terminated by the sequence '/*' in columns 1 and 2. However, by including an alternative argument in the DD statement the input could have been taken from a dataset on disc. Catalog procedures can also take arguments like macros, and so form a powerful way of disguising the horrors of JCL.

8.5.3 Operating system control languages

In the IBM environment, batch jobs are controlled by JCL and interactive work is done using the Time Sharing Option (TSO) which has its own command syntax, quite different from JCL. (An experienced observer has likened computing with TSO to 'kicking a dead whale along the beach'.) When ICL were planning the software for their new 2900 range in the early seventies they decided to avoid this incompatibility by having a single command language, SCL, that could be used in identical form in both batch and interactive modes. An example of SCL is given in Fig. 8.2.

Before embarking on an explanation of Fig. 8.2, some background information is in order. The architectural conception of the 2900 series is based on a procedural stack, and the system is designed with the efficient execution of block structured languages in mind. The operating system (VME) is written in a high-level block structured language, S3, which has much in common with Algol 68, and all system calls take the form of procedure calls. (VME is an 'in-process architecture of the type discussed in Chapter 3 and elsewhere in this book.) This procedural concept extends into the system control language. Although it is not apparent from the example given, SCL is a fully-fledged block-structured high-level language. User programs are regarded as procedures and are activated by a procedure call; indeed, one of the early ICL manuals stated (in paraphrase) that 'the solution to the problem is expressed in SCL; where facilities not provided by SCL are required, a procedure written by the user in a different language may be called'. In the same way, system activity is initiated by a procedure call, the main difference being that actual parameters are identified by keyword, rather than by position as in most programming languages.

With this background we can now look at Fig. 8.2. This is (more or less) the SCL for a simple file update operation, incorporating vetting of the transaction file before updating. It is assumed that the programs DATAVET, SORT UPDATE and PRINT have already been compiled, and are held in the user's file directory in the communal file store.

The SCL starts with a job header (for accounting purposes), and immediately declares a local variable MESSAGE, of type STRING. The procedure INPUT__FILE reads data from the SCL stream and places it in a named file; the actual data ('alien data') is enclosed in the 'brackets' '- - - -' and '++++'. Compare the 'DD* . . . /*' construct in JCL.) 'ASSIGN__FILE' is a system procedure that establishes a connection between a named actual file and a 'local name' to be used within a program to access a file. 'WORK__FILE' creates a new temporary file, which just has a local name. By default, it will be of standard format and located on disc. 'DATAVET(YES)' calls the DATAVET procedure: it is

```
JOB (NAME = SALES.UPDATE)
STRING MESSAGE
INPUT   FILE(NAME = SALES)
- - - -

<cards detailing transactions>

+ + + +
ASSIGN__FILE(NAME = SALES, LNAME = UPDATES)
WORK   FILE(NAME = ERRORS)
DATAVET(YES)
IF MESSAGE = "ERRORS FOUND" THEN
     LISTFILE(NAME = ERRORS, COPIES = 2) FI
WORK__FILE(LNAME = SORTED, DESC = *STDMT)
SORT
ASSIGN   FILE(NAME = STOCK, LNAME = MASTER)
NEW__FILE(NAME =STOCK(+1)
ASSIGN__FILE(NAME = STOCK, LNAME = NEWMASTER, ACCESS = W)
UPDATE
SAVE__FILE(NAME = STOCK)
WORK__FILE(NAME = SUMMARY)
PRINT
ENDJOB
* * * *
```

Fig. 8.2 Example of SCL.

assumed that this expects one argument, which in this call is the string 'YES'. It is also assumed that the program will assign a value to the variable 'MESSAGE'. This value is tested by the IF statement (note the terminating FI, Algol 68-style) to determine if the errors file should be printed. Another temporary file is created for the SORT program; note the second parameter * STDMT, which specifies the file to have standard magnetic tape format (compare the use to a system-defined DDNAME in JCL). After sorting the updating starts. A new master file is created (the name 'STOCK(+1)' denotes a file called stock with a generation number one greater than that of the last version of STOCK). This is assigned to the local name 'NEWMASTER' with write access, and after the update it is made permanent. Finally some printing takes place and the job ends.

This example does not bring out explicitly the block-structured nature of SCL, because for the sake of user-convenience, whenever a user program is called (e.g. DATAVET) the compiler encloses the call in BEGIN . . . END brackets. These brackets serve to control resource allocation: files created or assigned take effect at the next BEGIN, and are de-allocated (along with all other resources used by a program) at the matching END. A further application of block structure is that the whole SCL program is enclosed by the system in an 'outer SCL' block which serves to set default values for various parameters and to define a number of system variables that all programs expect to find.

SCL was a brave experiment, like the rest of the 2900 series bringing 'state of the art' ideas into a system for everyday use. It cannot be accounted an unqualified success. For batch work it is probably no worse than JCL, though experience shows that users do not appreciate the subtleties implicit in the use of block structure for resource allocation. For interactive use it falls into the TSO category (kicking a dead whale along the beach). Making all commands into procedure calls increases the amount of typing that is required to get anything done, and the block structuring is just pain – interactive use of a computer system is very difficult once the user gets knee-deep in nested begin . . . end pairs.

8.5.4   Machine-independent operating systems

When operating systems first appeared as an integral part of computer systems in the mid-1960s they were regarded as extensions of the hardware, and it was accepted that they had to be highly machine-specific. As experience was gained dissatisfaction with this state of affairs became apparent, especially as the growing use of high-level programming languages was introducing an element of machine-independence into programs. Out of this dissatisfaction grew the demand for a universal job-control language, and many national and international bodies (ANSI, CODASYL, BCS . . .) set to work to define such a language. For all one knows, they are at it still, though their efforts have been overtaken by events. Experience shows that attempts by international bodies to impose standards in computing from above almost always fail; the standards that stick tend to be those that develop from the grass roots because a language or system is found to be peculiarly suited to its purpose, and is widely available. Early in computing history FORTRAN became a *de facto* standard for just such reasons; later, Pascal followed the same path. In the operating system world the convenience of UNIX, coupled with its portability, seem set to make it the primary contender as the first standard operating system for anything bigger than an 8-bit micro. Users of these latter classes of machine have already standardized on CP/M and MS-DOS, and in the mainframe world the dominance of IBM and IBM-compatible hardware makes JCL an approximation to a standard. Increasingly, end users will not see the operating system as we know it today – they will work in an integrated software environment (as, for example, that provided by the SMALLTALK system, or the Apple LISA.) However, system developers will still use operating systems. The optimists are learning UNIX, and the pessimists are struggling with JCL.

Further reading

OPERATING SYSTEMS IN GENERAL

Although there are many books available, the rapidly changing nature of the subject means that the older ones are not really relevant to the current generation of systems. Some modern books that are in line with the approach of this book are:

Theaker, C.J. and Brookes, G.R. (1983), *A Practical Course on Operating Systems*, Macmillan, London.

Calingaert, P. (1982) *Operating System Elements: A user perspective*, Prentice Hall, Englewood Cliffs, NJ.

Deitel, H.M. (1983) *An Introduction to Operating Systems*, Addison Wesley, Reading, Mass.

Lister, A.M. (1979) *Fundamentals of Operating Systems*, Macmillan, London.

All of these are interesting reading. Deitel's book includes case studies of many widely-used systems, and is particularly recommended.

IBM OPERATING SYSTEMS

A good account of these mainframe systems is given in

Davis, W.S. (1983) *Operating Systems: A systematic view*, Addison Wesley, Reading, Mass.

For masochists who wish to plumb the depths of IBM Job Control Language,

Brown, G. de W. (1977) *System 370 Job Control Language*, Wiley, New York.

is an invaluable companion.

CP/M

Most of the CP/M books on the shelves are 'noddy's guides' to using the system. Three which go a bit further into the actual working of CP/M are:

Murtha, S.M. and Waite, M. (1983) *CP/M Primer*, Wiley, New York.
Waite, M. and Lafore, P. (1983) *Soul of CP/M*, Howard W. Sams, Indianapolis.
Johnson-Laird, A. (1983) *The Programmer's CP/M Handbook*, Osborne/McGraw Hill,
    Berkeley, California.

UNIX

The inner workings of UNIX are a closely guarded secret of A.T. and T.'s Bell
Laboratories, so the available books do not give much detail. If you want to know
more about the system from the user's point of view the following are highly
recommended:

Brown, P.J. (1984) *Starting with INIX*, Addison Wesley, London.
Bourne, S.R. (1983) *The UNIX System*, Addison Wesley, Reading, Mass.
Kernighan, B.W. and Pike, R. (1984) *The UNIX Programming Environment*, Prentice
    Hall, Englewood Cliffs, NJ.
Banahan M. and Rutter A. (1982) *UNIX – The Book*, Sigma Technical Press,
    Wilmslow

VAX/VMS

An overview of VAX/VMS operation is to be found in:

Levy, H.M. and Eckhouse, R.H. Jr. (1980) *Computer Programming and Architecture*:
    The VAX11, Digital Press, Bedford, Mass.

Alternatively,

Kenah, L.J. and Bate, S.F. (1984) *VAX/VMS Internals and Data Structures*, Digital
    Press, Bedford, Mass.

will tell you much more about VAX/VMS than you will ever want to know.

Index